W9-CNL-101

INVITATIONS

INVITATIONS

MARC  FRIEDLAND

Text by Betty Goodwin

Photographs by Susan Salinger

Styled by Valorie Hart

Clarkson Potter/Publishers
New York

Grateful acknowledgment is made for permission to reprint invitations from *Amelia Earheart: The Final Flight*, *Hope*, *The Hunchback*, *In Search of Dr. Seuss*, and *Kingfish: The Story of Huey P. Long* provided by Turner Pictures Worldwide and Turner Network Television; the invitation from "A Time for Heroes," which was generously underwritten; and to reprint Dr. Seuss text and figures, trademarks and copyrights of Dr. Seuss Enterprises, L.P. All rights reserved. Used by consent.

Published by Clarkson N. Potter/Publishers,
201 East 50th Street, New York, New York 10022.
Member of the Crown Publishing Group.

Random House, Inc. New York, Toronto, London, Sydney, Auckland
www.randomhouse.com

CLARKSON N. POTTER, POTTER, and colophon
are trademarks of Clarkson N. Potter, Inc.

Printed in China

DESIGNED BY BRIDGETTE KLOECKER AND BRYON LOMAS
for CREATIVE INTELLIGENCE, INC., LA

Library of Congress Cataloging-in-Publication Data
Friedland, Marc.
     Invitations / by Marc Friedland : text by Betty
  Goodwin ; photography by Susan Salinger. — 1st ed.
     1. Entertaining—Planning. 2. Invitation cards. I. Goodwin,
Betty. II. Title.
GV1472.F75   1998   98-9182
395.4—dc21   CIP
ISBN 0-609-60303-5

10 9 8 7 6 5 4 3 2 1

First Edition

DEDICATION

To Mom, "Jean Marlow"

who combined chartreuse and navy long before I was
born and whose flair for style brightens every room

And in loving/living memory of:

Dr. Robert Gould

who taught me how to combine
my creativity and intelligence

To John Ries

who encouraged me to create my first invitation

And to my dad, Joseph

who instilled in me the understanding
that quality is everything

CONTENTS
{from beginning to end}

INTRODUCTION

A CAPTIVATING INVITATION creates a sense of anticipation and drama. It sets the tone and spirit of the event to come. It is tactile and emotional. In social circles, it can be the determining factor in who accepts and who declines. Most important, an invitation beckoning friends and families to a joyous celebration or announcing an important rite of passage reflects the personality of the sender and a sense of occasion, whether it is a fairy-tale wedding, a Hollywood premiere, an annual museum gala, or simply an intimate dinner for friends.

Ever since I was a boy, I cherished the excitement of checking the mailbox for the envelopes and packages addressed to me. Even in the era of lightning-fast communication, I still feel the same way. Now I try to convey to my clients the power of transforming a flat medium into a limitless means of social communication. An invitation printed on white paper with black ink that states the facts and figures of time, date, and place is perfectly adequate. However, when the vocabulary of communication combines words, colors, textures, images, and materials, something magical happens.

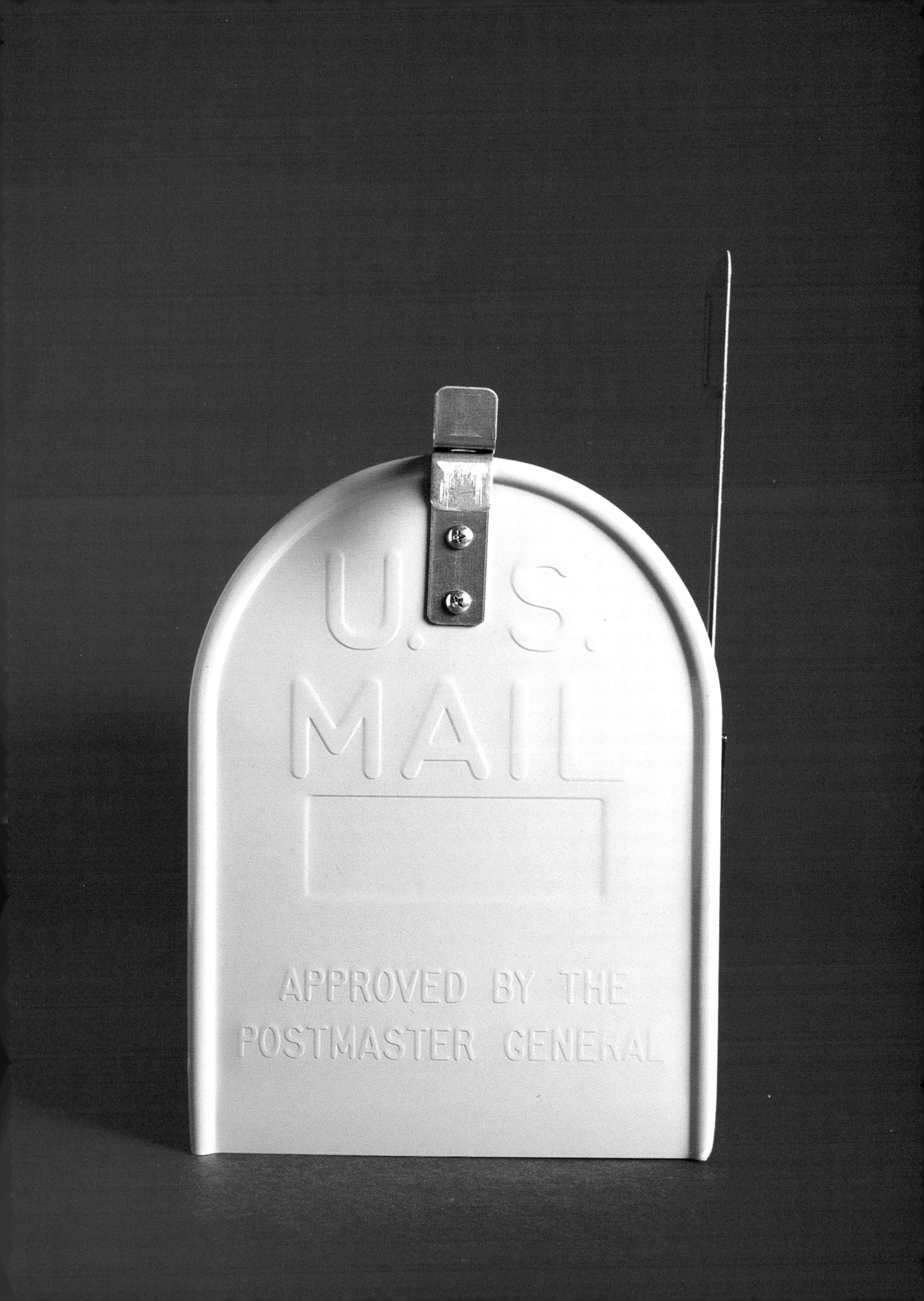
U.S.
MAIL
APPROVED BY THE
POSTMASTER GENERAL

INVITATIONS...

It is the combination of these elements that turns designing and creating an invitation into an art form, one that is accessible to everyone. The variables are infinite: since each event defines its own parameters, and every individual possesses a unique character, it is possible to create a distinct sensory experience for both the sender and the receiver.

Tradition has its time and place, but it's hard to believe that until recently, people who selected invitations and announcements for the most meaningful occasions in their lives felt obliged to follow certain social dictums, such as "appropriate" format, paper size, and color, "correct" wording, and the way to fold the paper, insert it into the envelope, and even address the envelope.

Amazing invitations can be fashioned from almost any imaginable material. A favorite chintz can be used to line an envelope; beautiful buttons or old-world sealing wax can work as unusual closures; handmade papers from around the world, such as delicate Japanese rice papers, papers embedded with seashell fragments, flowers, or shredded newspaper, even vintage wrapping paper found at local swap meets, provide the textural backdrop. Each possesses its own unique characteristics and style; each imparts a particular sentiment.

An invitation can be written as a narrative, worded with humor, or penned in verse. One of the most original and delightful announcements that I worked on sprang from just a few words—to this day I know them by heart. It was a birth announcement in honor of the daughter of actress and writer Carrie Fisher. Far from the traditional wording of "We are pleased to announce . . . ," the announce-

ment, whose imagery included inspiration from an old book of nursery rhymes and songs, read: "Someone summered in my stomach. Someone's fallen through my legs. To make an infant omelet, simply scramble sperm and eggs."

Lettering styles have their own particular character when they are representative of a distinguishable era, be it a 1940s Art Deco typeface or the pre—computer age charm of an old Smith Corona typewriter. For romance and prestige, nothing compares to the elegance of a quill pen dipped into gold ink and scripted into the most beautiful calligraphy.

Never underestimate the importance of the envelope. Consider the way in which it unfolds, the manner in which it is addressed, stamped, and perhaps delivered. To invite friends to an Academy Awards viewing party, an executive from Radio City Music Hall had his invitations—an assemblage of a real clapper board, popcorn, and plastic hot dogs all contained in an authentic film canister "envelope"—dispatched by messengers dressed in old usher uniforms. Another innovative client arranged for the hand delivery of his child's storybook-themed birthday invitations by messengers dressed as fairy-tale characters.

You can have fun seeing how far you can go with what fits inside of an envelope. One of my first corporate special events was the launch of the seedless watermelon to New York's most discerning food critics. For the rooftop garden luncheon, I instinctively knew that an engraved ecru card just wouldn't do. Instead, to create a buzz about this unusual product introduction, I crafted the invitations from AstroTurf, red-and-white checked tablecloths, and wicker.

It was from this first type of innovative design that

my Los Angeles–based company, Creative Intelligence, Inc., was born. Through the years, my dedicated staff and I have experimented with virtually every size, shape, and form of invitation imaginable, for every type of occasion and event, addressing every nuance of personal and corporate communication. There have been couples who pooled their funds to create the perfect wedding, parents who celebrated the joy of welcoming a new baby, people who marked a milestone birthday. There have been intimate dinner parties for some of the biggest names in Hollywood, grand soirees tossed by some of the nation's most famous hosts, and galas commemorating events for some of the most prestigious institutions and corporations. And judging by the buzz created and the rapid and positive R.S.V.P. rates, the invitations have played an integral role in the parties' successes.

I have written this book to inspire you to look differently at the materials in your world, to create from the passion found within you, and to go beyond the store-bought mentality. In the pages that follow, I will take you through the process I use daily, providing you with some technical foundation, vivid examples of our work, and a wide range of ideas. Perhaps you will make your own invitations, or you will use this book as a guide to encourage your own stationer or printer to execute some fresh ideas. My hope is that you will never need to resort to using the phone, fax, or Internet to summon your friends together for life's momentous events. That is definitely an invitation "don't."

I "most cordially invite you," "request the honor of your presence," and with "no regrets" accepted, welcome you to the world of celebration—the celebration of life!

An Offbeat Verse
penned by actress, writer, and mother-to-be Carrie Fisher is combined with an illustration inspired from a book of antique nursery rhymes, which joyfully announced the birth of her first child, a baby girl.

YOU CAN'T REFUSE

HANDMADE PAPERS,

whether they contain natural inclusions such as flowers or
straw or are hand-dyed with saturated pigments, provide
the basis for a compelling invitation.

THE BASICS

1

DETERMINING THE FEELING an invitation conveys is much like building a house. The foundation includes the theme of an event, the host's personal style, and the degree of formality—from a sit-down dinner to a picnic in the garden. The size, look, and elaborateness—or simplicity—of an invitation should be commensurate with the nature of the gathering. Although everyone brings a different perspective to an event, no one should be afraid to experiment or break convention—keeping in mind that more doesn't necessarily mean better. Not only is an over-the-top assemblage that is hand-messengered to guests unnecessary for a casual two-hour cocktail party, but it would give the wrong idea about an event meant to be informal and fun. Additionally, most people would agree that overly elaborate charity invitations send the wrong message.

when created in monochromatic tones of whites and cream, reflect an understated elegance and style.

INDUSTRIAL PAPERS,
such as corrugated cardboard or everyday brown kraft paper, are ideal for those events that have an urban sensibility.

If there is no obvious theme to a party, sometimes the setting itself creates the theme, such as the architecture of the house where the gathering is taking place; or, if the party is at the beach, nature itself might provide the inspiration in the form of pale blues and whites.

There are many ways invitations are used to engage and pique the interest of would-be guests. To summon friends to his wife's fortieth birthday celebration—a week-long cruise off the coast of Italy—a Hollywood studio executive sent out invitations that were actual itineraries of the twelve-day voyage. Inspired by a captain's travelog, each day's entry described the events that would unfold from sunup to sundown. It was packaged inside a nautical-looking folio covered in cotton duck and edged with navy piping. Another client, a high-tech billionaire, notified friends of a masquerade ball he was staging in an Italian twelfth-century palazzo by enclosing the essential information in a burgundy velvet–covered box containing a handmade feathered mask, which served as both a gift and an invitation.

Even on a modest budget, inspiration can be drawn from virtually anywhere: travel destinations, museums, decorating styles, fashion magazines, favorite movies, styles of a bygone era, old books. Think about the colors, textures, and, of course, the words that reflect your personality. A few years ago, after being away on location for several months, actor Alec Baldwin gave a small party at his home. "Come over and have dinner with me before I leave town again!" read his invitation, rustic and earthy-looking, calligraphed in a simple print on handmade paper fashioned from fallen bark layered with a bold, graphic batik pattern. It seemed to perfectly communicate to his friends that they could look forward to having a great night, relaxing and casual, and certainly not stuffy. To make his guests feel even more at home, in the bottom right-hand corner he added "Feel free to bring a guest."

{ALL ABOUT PAPER}

With hundreds and thousands of paper types to choose from, the selection of paper stock is the first step in determining the tone of an invitation. Paper creates a mood and helps communicate the right message. For example, invitations for a fund-raising dinner benefiting the Save the Rain Forest Foundation used 100 percent cotton rag paper and noted on the reverse: "No trees were destroyed to create this paper."

Papers are made either by hand or by machine. The more unusual the paper, the more expensive it tends to be. For elegance, the best selection is 100 percent cotton fiber paper, also known as cotton rag, which has a superb affinity for ink and is amenable to a wide variety of printing processes. Papers come in different weights and thicknesses, ranging from tissue thin to a heavy 600-pound card stock, which has a wonderful "meaty" thickness. Thick stock conveys substance and is the ideal medium for commemorative announcements and important rites of passage, while lighter-weight stocks, such as parchments and tissues, add a delicate element to the presentation of birth announcements and wedding invitations.

Another distinguishing feature of paper is its finish, including silky smooth, velvety matte, polished glossy, shiny cast-coated, and linen finish. Handmade papers, which are often made from natural organic materials including cotton rag, hemp, and plant fibers, have been produced for thousands of years

NATURAL DECKLED EDGES,
the signature of the centuries-old process of paper making, have an old-world European sense of luxury.

DOODADS

& DECKLED

and are direct descendants of papyrus, the earliest known paper, fabricated from an aquatic plant growing in the Nile Valley. Many handmade papers still originate in small villages around the world, and each has its own distinctive features, such as banana fiber paper from Costa Rica, bamboo particle paper from Thailand, and many eclectic varieties coming from Japan. Inherently irregular in texture, especially when dried flowers, leaves, or other "inclusions" are involved, handmade papers tend to be used mostly for decoration, such as lining an envelope, since printing directly onto them is often difficult.

Yet another category of papers that lend themselves to a stylized look are the specialty or decorative papers. Marbled papers, which are still being made by hand primarily in Italy and England, were originally used in the exquisite art of bookbinding. Vellum papers provide an air of drama and softness when layered over photographs or simply used as an overlay containing a favorite poem or quotation. For dazzling effects, there are colorful Mylar, glitter, and holographic papers.

Recycled and industrial papers—including kraft paper—are used more and more because they convey a relaxed and informal urban look and are environmentally friendly. However, not all recycled papers look the same. More and more fine papers today have a high recycled fiber content and are indistinguishable from virgin papers.

Papers come in virtually every color of the rainbow, including a vast range of whites, from the brightest whites to creamy ecrus. Just as color palettes change in fashion, the same holds true with regard to paper. At one time, stationery for invitations was limited to white, cream, or soft pastels, but today, the range is much wider, from saturated shades like mustard and eggplant to muted tones of khaki, taupe, and celadon.

EDGES

{ADDRESSING}

GUIDELINES FOR ADDRESSING ENVELOPES ARE NOT CARVED IN STONE. THESE WORK FOR MOST PEOPLE.
THE BOTTOM LINE IS THAT YOU SHOULD DO WHAT MAKES YOU AND YOUR GUESTS MOST COMFORTABLE.

WHOSE NAME FIRST

It is customary never to separate the husband's first name from his surname. MR. AND MRS. JOHN SMITH could also be addressed as JANE AND JOHN SMITH, but not JOHN AND JANE SMITH.

If a married woman has retained her given name, it is standard for her name to come first. If two people are living together but are not married, their names should be written on two separate lines, with the woman's name appearing first. Or they can be written together on one line as MS. MARY GREEN AND MR. JOHN SMITH.

ADDRESSING FOR SAME-SEX COUPLES

For same-sex couples, if you know both partners equally well, their names should be written in alphabetical order on two separate lines. If you know only one person well, list that person's name first.

INVITING GUESTS

If you are inviting someone with a guest whose name you don't know, be sure to include AND GUEST after the recipient's name. Otherwise it is understood that the invitation is only for the person whose name appears on the invitation. For women, AND ESCORT can also be used, though it is somewhat old-fashioned.

If you are inviting someone with a guest whose name you know, your friend's name should go first. Even though a woman's name usually precedes a man's, in this situation your friend John Smith's name will appear first, as in MR. JOHN SMITH AND MS. MARY GREEN.

INVITING CHILDREN

Invitations to girls under age eighteen should be addressed MISS JANE SMITH. For ages eighteen and over, MS. is preferred. Boys under age nine are MASTER. Between ages nine and seventeen, no title is used. At eighteen, MR. is used.

INVITING FAMILIES

When inviting families, when the children's names are not known or when there are more than three children, you can write MR. AND MRS. JOHN SMITH AND FAMILY. When the children's names are known, use first names only, in order of age, starting with the oldest, as in MR. AND MRS. JOHN SMITH, EMILY, SAMANTHA, AND AARON.

INVITING DIVORCÉES AND WIDOWS

Divorcées can be MS. JANE GREEN (maiden name) or MRS. JANE GREEN (married name). In the past, widows were addressed as MRS. JOHN SMITH, but today, MRS. MARY SMITH is acceptable.

USING TITLES

Business titles like senior vice president generally should not be used on social invitations. The exceptions are for medical doctors and honorifics such as mayor, judge, and ambassador, as well as military personnel. If a married couple includes a woman doctor, write DR. MARY GREEN AND MR. JOHN SMITH. If both are doctors, use THE DOCTORS SMITH OR DRS. JANE AND JOHN SMITH.

and Mrs. Stewart Schl...
23034 Park Dulce
...abasas, California
9   3   0

Mr. Bryon Lomas
8497 Sunset Boulevard, Suite 18
Los Angeles, California
9   0   0   6   9

Valorie De Sica
World Talent Agency
6000 Beverly, Suite 600
Hollywood, California
9   0   0   6   9

...& Mrs. Bill Clinton
...Pennsylvania Avenue
Northwest
Washington, D.C.
2   0   5   0   0

Mr. and Mrs. Rubén Esparz...
125 Paseo De Gracia
Madrid, Spain

CALLIGRAPHIC ADDRESSING,
done in a variety of hands and colors, can make the most
simplistic invitation a memorable keepsake. 21

Each typeface or font—the design of letters or numerals—has its own distinct character. Just as childlike scribbles are inappropriate for *formal invitations*, the importance of choosing the **right typeface** for the right function should never be underestimated. There are two basic forms of lettering: *hand-done calligraphy* and ELECTRONIC or mechanical typesetting.

Typefaces are usually named after the DESIGNERS who **created** them, as with the CLASSIC sixteenth-century face **Garamond**, the sophisticated **Bodoni** and **Caslon**, and the modern, 1930s-designed **Gill**.

Type size is measured in points. Varying the point size and adding a **SECOND** typeface can create additional **I M P A C T .** Keep in mind that it is COUNTERPRODUCTIVE if the typeface is *Too Elaborate* or if the point size is too small –eight points or less– to read. Sometimes the beauty and refinement of hand *scripting* will suffice only for the addressing of an envelope or the contents of the most formal invitation. Most people think of calligraphy as a scrawl with *Curlicues and Flourishes*, but a skilled calligrapher may have up to twenty or twenty-five "hands." While COMPUTER-GENERATED calligraphy is readily available, it simply does not take the place of the inherent **imPerfe ctions** and BEAUTY of *handwritten work*.

aqua tonic	tang	lime
robin's egg	brick	fab fuchsia
Nantucket blue	tamale	creamy buttah
lavender	saffron	sage
aubergine	garnet	Emerald City
basic black	champagne	gray rosé

THE WRITE COLOR OF INK

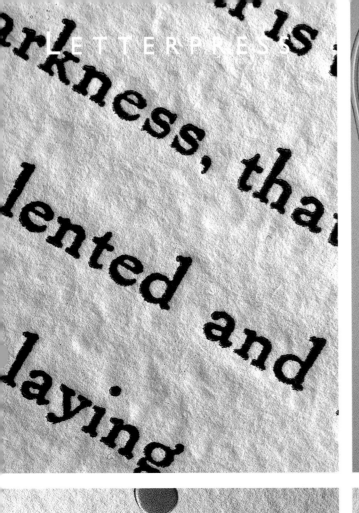
LETTERPRESS

BLIND EMBOSSING

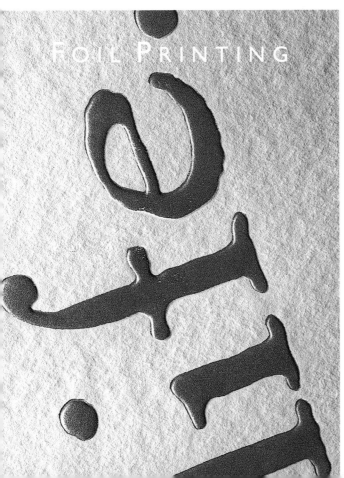
FOIL PRINTING

ENGRAVING

{PRINTING METHODS}

Since cost, time, paper stock, quantity, and style all go into choosing the right printing method, it is important to know the types available. For example, a very textured handmade paper is difficult to put through a traditional printing press and would be better suited to the mechanics of letterpress printing, an old-fashioned method that entails forming letters into a metal stamping die.

Using a hand-etched plate, engraving is considered the finest method of printing because it captures the most detail—U.S. currency is a perfect example. It is also the most labor-intensive and expensive. Photoengraving produces the same results through a different process of etching.

A quick alternative to engraving is thermography, which creates a raised image and is far less expensive since it doesn't require the fabrication of a cast-metal die. Offset lithography is the quickest and most economical method of printing and can be accomplished at your local print shop; this process can be done in virtually any color ink, from metallic to fluorescent, and on virtually any size of paper. Keep in mind, though, that the larger the paper and the more colors, the greater the expense.

Embossing is a technique that raises the surface of paper to create letters or a design such as a crest, while blind embossing is the same process without ink. Foil stamping creates eye-catching designs with shiny metallic or pigmented foil.

Printing inks are specified by the Pantone Matching System, which allows designers and printers to specify and ensure color consistency. Be aware that colors look different depending on paper stocks and surfaces.

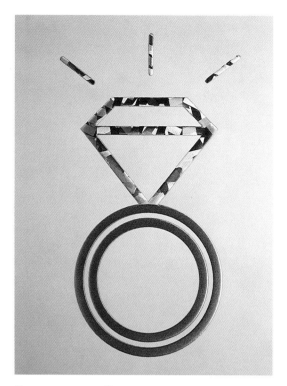

DAZZLING FOIL
transforms this wedding shower invitation into a sparkling diamond with a holographic faceted finish.

ETCHED METAL DIES,
used for engraving or letterpress printing, have intricacy and detail that only this form of printing can accomplish.

23

R.S.V.P. CARDS

are a modern convenience and can range in style depending on the nature of the event. Personalizing them with the guest's name adds a touch of style and informs the host who has responded should someone forget to include his or her name.

{COMPONENTS}

An invitation "ensemble" often consists of several elements in addition to the main invitation. These elements are intended to communicate information clearly to guests. They should be smaller than the actual invitation so they don't detract from it, and should be used judiciously so guests will not have to grapple with too many pieces of paper.

A reception card tells the location and time of the reception when it is to take place at a different location from the primary event, such as with weddings and Bar Mitzvahs.

Today, the R.S.V.P. card is the social norm. However, responding by telephone is certainly acceptable for informal social gatherings and business functions and should be indicated with a phone number and contact person on the lower left corner of the main invitation. Prior to the introduction of the R.S.V.P. card, guests were expected to accept or decline an invitation on their own personal stationery, virtually rewriting by hand all pertinent

PLACE CARDS

at formal functions should be beautifully calligraphed and coordinate with the table setting or menu.

details. Now the R.S.V.P. card functions like a form letter with either boxes to check or lines to fill in, and it can be personalized with a guest's name scripted by hand. Definitely the most appealing option is a blank card, save for a line across the bottom reading: "The favour of a reply is requested." (Note the Old English spelling of favor, which is recommended for formal events.) This allows guests adequate space to send back their response with a handwritten note. For informal parties, nicely designed postcards have become popular and save the cost of an additional envelope. Direction cards are included for out-of-town guests or for when a venue is difficult to find.

Other inserts include a card requesting a donation to a specific charity in lieu of a gift. Out-of-town guests may be sent itineraries of events for celebrations lasting several days with a rundown of things to do while in town, as well as a list of suggested hotels. Sheer tissue paper inserts that once served to protect long-drying engraver's inks from rubbing off onto other components are strictly a decorative embellishment now. When the tissue inserts are handmade or printed with a favorite quotation, they convey a sense of style or help set the mood more poetically.

Although separate from the invitation, save-the-date cards are now common. Mailed as much as six months ahead of time, save-the-dates are useful when the guest list includes people with very busy schedules or when the date falls during a holiday season. However, you must be sure of your guest list because it is a terrible faux pas to not follow up with an invitation, should you later change your mind about inviting someone.

ESCORT CARDS,
also known as table seating cards, show the guest's name on the front with his or her table assignment on the reverse.

SMALL, UNSEALED,
and calligraphed envelopes, containing a card with the table number, are another traditional approach to the use of escort cards.

{USING CALLIGRAPHY}

Hand-done calligraphy requires the mastery of an artist, the precision of a surgeon, and the ability to work within the most demanding deadlines. When choosing a calligrapher, aside from the beauty of a personal touch and the meticulousness of the work, consider the practical issues of timeliness and accuracy. An accomplished calligrapher should be available for last-minute changes, additions, and, when the final R.S.V.P.s come in, scribing table numbers, escort cards, and place cards. Calligraphers charge by the address or the line, so keep this in mind when comparing prices; correcting their mistakes at no additional charge is a standard practice but should be confirmed in advance.

When selecting a calligrapher, ask for samples of the person's work on your chosen envelopes. A skilled calligrapher should be adept at mixing ink colors to match your printed ink, ribbon, or fabric. And be sure that the selected hand is appropriate for the invitation style. Scripts that are too fanciful can be impossible to read. The guest list for the calligrapher should be very legible and in a three-line format. Don't expect flawless accuracy, always double-check the work, and pad deadlines by a few days.

If friends with budding calligraphy skills offer a gift of calligraphy, approach this gesture of kindness with caution. Too often, the stress from working with a well-intentioned amateur compounded with the normal matrimonial anxieties makes envelope addressing a major source of frustration. Suggest, instead, that the calligrapher-friend help inscribe the escort cards, place cards, or table numbers.

{ALL ABOUT ENVELOPES}

If an envelope catches someone's attention by the way it looks and feels, or even by how it is addressed and stamped, the stack of mail piled on a desk or in a mailbox can wait. Because presentation is so important, many envelopes are now custom-crafted through a process called die-cutting, resulting in envelopes of any size, shape, and material. At Creative Intelligence, we have an inventory of well over two hundred dies—masses of different squares and rectangles, to be sure, as well as rhomboids and envelopes shaped like bongo drums or kites.

Envelopes, of course, can be made of any material, as long as the surface is suitable for writing on and the material is sturdy enough to protect the invitation and survive delivery. Clear plastics and vellum that show part of an invitation can be especially powerful. Indeed, the term "envelope" should be defined loosely as anything that can contain a message. For example, a plastic baby bottle makes a fine envelope for a birth announcement. Many equally dramatic effects can be made through the selection of paper, material, printing process, and ornate addressing.

Inner envelopes, which tend to be used for traditional invitations, are no longer required for an elegant impression. However, for certain events, such as a formal wedding, they look best with just a guest's name written across them.

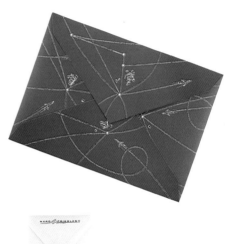

the ENVELOPES
please

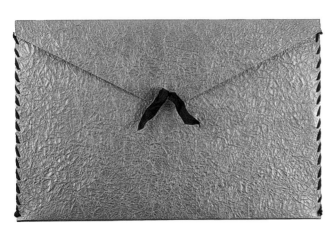

Come join us and munch
with the Peter Rabbit bunch
When we Shower
Andrea
Baby Shower Lunch
10th is the date
don't be late
the spot
Potter loc

NOSTALGIC PAPER,
buttons, and bows along with rhyming text are the
whimsical touches that set the stage for this
charming shower for a baby boy.

Hello World

2

WHAT BETTER WAY to capture the wonder of life and the promise of the future than through the rituals welcoming a newborn into the world. Birth announcements as well as invitations to the rites and celebrations associated with the arrival of a new life can express the richness of the occasion and become precious family treasures.

It takes thoughtfulness to find the right expression. While it's possible to be too cute, try to avoid the overly staid and formal—after all, it is for a baby. And what parents consider funny may very well not amuse anyone else. Thankfully, color choice has progressed outside of the conventions of pink for girls and blue for boys. In fact, avoid all clichés, especially loud, boastful ones. Sending a bubble gum cigar and the message, "It's a boy" feels quite impersonal. And since a child is

LILLIAN DIONE MARSHALL

GLAMOROUS AND UNEXPECTED

is the hand-tinted photograph, ABOVE, used to announce the arrival of the daughter of producers Kathleen Kennedy and Frank Marshall. The booklike announcement, BELOW, was the ideal format to welcome the twin sons of Adrienne and Seth Friedland. Shoe designer Kenneth Cole and wife Maria Cuomo Cole put their newborn's best foot forward, OPPOSITE, by incorporating their daughter's first footprint in her announcement.

JORDAN MARSHA
FRIDAY, JULY 15TH 1994
7 LBS.

EVAN HARRIS
...IDAY, JULY 15TH, 1994
5 LBS. ~ 9 OZ.

TWINS

an original unlike any other, it is important to treat him or her as an individual; avoid the tendency to ascribe a predetermined personality, such as a baseball player or a ballerina, in the choice of elements.

Memorable announcements should evoke soft, precious images with a nostalgic feeling reminiscent of a simpler time. Even the dimensions of the card reflect the fragility of a baby since they tend to be diminutive rather than oversized and excessive. Colors have an antique aura, such as celadon, aqua, dusty rose, or gold. Materials are ethereal, such as a beautiful wired French ribbon tied around fine tissue paper that "diapers" the announcement. An elegant wrapping paper or fabric depicting whimsical characters or animals makes for a charming backdrop. Black-and-white or sepia-toned photographs as well as hand-tinted prints imbue a timeless, elegant quality, especially when processed on a pearl- or satin-finish paper.

Since people are starting their families at an older age, the design of babies' cards is becoming distinctly more sophisticated. The parents' taste and sensibilities tend to be clearly defined and, often, more understated. Many couples also hope to reflect the unique character of the family into which the baby is entering. Shoe designer Kenneth Cole and his wife Maria loved the idea of showing an imprint of their newborn's feet, which was the main design element on their simple, elegant announcement.

Wording for announcements tends to be very simple. The parents' names followed by the baby's name can suffice. When there are other children in the family, it's nice to include their names: "Diane, David, and Michael Beveridge joyfully announce the

&

Maria, Kenneth, Emily and Amanda

joyfully welcome

Catherine Camilla Cole

the PITTER-PATTER of little FEET

The well-versed correspondent begins training at an early age. In fact, as soon as a baby is born, he or she should have personalized stationery so that Mom or Dad can write notes in style.

Thank-you notes for shower or birth gifts don't have to be very large; a small, 4-by-5-inch panel card can hold all that needs to be said. Using the baby's first name only or the first and last names is equally popular and appropriate. Many parents like to choose colors and typefaces that match their child's birth announcements, although that isn't a necessity.

First sets of stationery can range from sur-prisingly sophisticated to wonderfully playful, old-fashioned-looking to extremely contemporary. To evoke innocence and Victorian style, ecru cards affixed with one dried, dusty pink sprig of larkspur befitted a baby girl and her slightly older sisters. Their names were each engraved across the top in gold by one of the Queen of England's calligraphers.

Another urbane solution was white, textured cards with a newborn boy's name blind-embossed in an informal script, torn around the edges and then collaged onto the top of the card. Envelopes, made from matching stock, featured the return address blind-embossed across the square flap back. More fanciful cards include a child's name accompanied by small images—perhaps an antique toy, doll, or fire truck—in papers and inks of crayon-bright colors.

Children's stationery can be used throughout the first few years as thank-you's, gift enclosures, or, perhaps, personal invitations to an informal tea party or play date! Whatever its function, giving chil-dren stationery teaches them about the importance of handwritten communication.

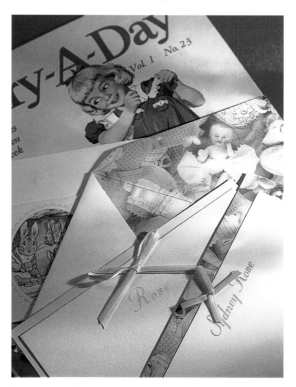

BABY'S FIRST NOTES
make a distinctive impression when the envelope is lined with nostalgic paper and layered, bordered cards are adorned with a petite satin bow.

birth of Jacqueline Marie." The birth day, date, and time as well as birth weight and sometimes the length are also commonly included, but it's more sophisti-cated to do without too many details. Another approach is to tie the birth to another special event —the holiday on which the child was born or a big change in the family's life. "We proudly announce an addition to our new home," read the birth announcement for Jason Reid Ginsburg, which coin-cided with his parents' move to a new house. The words appeared on a die-cut house which was wrapped in tissue paper and secured with a diaper pin. Attached to the pin was a small tag stating, "Our summer was a moving experience."

Being sensitive to special birth situations calls for creativity. I like to give twins equal billing with a book-like format that opens to reveal the details on separate, facing pages. Adopted children can be heralded with the parents "announcing the arrival of" or "joyfully welcoming" a baby. One single mother's announcement read, "Thank Heaven for Little Girls! Announcing with joy and love the birth of Melanie Alex."

Invitations to ceremonial baby namings and the Jewish bris (the latter is usually conveyed by phone because of the timing—eight days after a boy's birth) follow the same guidelines as birth announcements. If sending out both announcements and invitations seems daunting, selectively include an invitation printed on a simple vellum insert along with the announcement.

Superstitions aside, birth announcements and invitations can certainly be designed before a baby is born; a family member should notify a stationer with the particulars immediately after the birth. On a practical level, having the envelopes addressed and ready to mail can save time and stress. Generally, announcements are sent within two to three months of a baby's birth.

By sending birth announcements, most people simply wish to share their news and don't expect anything in return, but if the matter becomes an issue or seems uncomfortable, politely request "No gifts please" in the lower left-hand corner of a card.

As for the custom of throwing baby showers, it's no longer reserved for the girlfriends of the mother-to-be. And invitations reflect this as more and more showers honor the expectant couple as well as single parents, male and female. When a friend and I decided to throw a shower for a girlfriend who was giving birth to a boy, the invitation was a far cry from the usual stork and bundle. We chose a 1950s stock photo of a baby boy gleefully urinating. The caption read simply, "It's a baby shower!"

A BABY'S ARRIVAL and the move into a new home were combined in Carole and Michael Ginsburg's announcement, which was designed as a die-cut house and wrapped in a tissue diaper.

We proudly announce an addition to our new home

Our summer was a moving experience...

Please join us to shower the mama-to-be **Allison Robbins** with lots of guy stuff

Saturday, May 18 1:00 in the afternoon

It's a Baby Shower!

A COED BABY SHOWER given by the mother's two best male friends was announced using an irreverent '50s photo of a baby boy, old-fashioned typewriter-style typography, and bold, aqua tonic blue ink.

fiftieth-birthday invitations captured the Winklers' elegant
yet whimsical sense of style by topping all fifty blind-
embossed candles with gold-foil-embossed flames.

3

R E G A R D L E S S   O F   A G E, birthdays are a time to reflect and celebrate the wonder of being alive. Sharing these occasions with special friends and family makes it easy to gain inspiration for creating personal and meaningful invitations.

This is especially true of birthdays marking a milestone—from sixteen years old on up. Without a doubt, they are one of life's most irresistible opportunities for an anything-goes strategy, regardless of whether someone is planning an understated, homespun gathering or the birthday bash of a lifetime. Yet there is no escaping the fact that almost everyone feels differently about turning another year older. It doesn't matter if a person dreads broadcasting his or her age, enjoys the thirty-ninth yet one more time, or turns fifty with pride; the invitations can be designed to capture the essence of both the individual and the event with style and originality.

AN INVITATION TO TEA

on Old McDonald's farm, honoring Melanie Borinstein on her second birthday, above, reinterprets the tradition of the old-fashioned cloth-covered storybook format.

OPRAH WINFREY

summoned close friends and family to Stedman Graham's milestone birthday bash, with an elegant invitation, below, complete with a sepia-toned boyhood picture and an original quotation from Maya Angelou.

How this is done depends on whether the host is the celebrant, the party is being given in honor of someone else, or it is a surprise for some unsuspecting soul. The approach can be surprisingly low-key or wildly eccentric, with virtually anything in between.

Some people are very self-conscious about giving parties for themselves, in which case the communication can be as simple as calligraphy on interesting-textured paper exclaiming, "I'm turning thirty and I can't celebrate without you."

But perhaps the most memorable invitations are those that celebrate an individual's life—commemorating the journey he or she has traveled thus far. Whether in a lighthearted manner or with heartfelt sincerity, a birthday invitation is an ideal way to herald the guest of honor's personality and achievements. When Oprah Winfrey was planning Stedman Graham's forty-fifth birthday festivities, a very elegant fete held at the Theurer/Wrigley Mansion in Chicago, it was clearly meant to be a celebration of passage. But Oprah also wanted to convey the richness of Stedman's life, especially in the way he touched other people, so she chose to use a profound quotation—poetic words from her dear friend Maya Angelou. Centered and alone on the page, the quote read simply: "From a boy to a man/is not a distance/to measure/but the journey is hard/the destination is treasure." Beneath the printed overlay rested the invitation—a hunter-green card secured with a regal, aubergine, French-wired ribbon. It framed a portrait of Stedman as a young boy. Alongside the photo, the sentiment of the celebration was eloquently captured with the simple phrase, "Your presence would be treasured."

In a similar way, the use of a few well-chosen

The longer you blow
The longer you go

KENNY G'S

fortieth birthday invitation is austere in its presentation. Created from a natural white-rag stock and layered with the spice tones of Tahitian banana paper, the invitation is sealed with a Zen-inspired, origami-folded closure and completed with twig and raffia ties.

words expressed saxophonist Kenny G's joie de vivre on the invitations for his fortieth birthday party. "The longer you blow, the longer you go," read the Chinese-like proverb that dangled from a twig closure on the invitation's Zen-inspired outside wrapping. As the invitation opened, the musing continued, with guests invited to join in for an evening of "not-so-quiet reflection as Kenny blows the big four-O."

An invitation can also evoke a strong sense of personal style. When a young actress was about to turn twenty-one, she invited guests to her home for a "toast of champagne" in celebration of her reaching the legal drinking age. She expressed her level of taste and emerging sophistication through the use of a combination of materials, including a beautiful French eyelet lace used for the envelope lining and as a backdrop for a soft, celadon-green, deckle-edged card. What made it even more memorable was the suggestive hint of her favorite perfume, Joy. The fabric had been impregnated with the scent just before mailing.

Humor is another trait that can personalize an invitation. When Richard Moskowitz, a successful clothing manufacturer, was turning fifty, his wife Lisa knew that the invitation needed to capture his well-known jovial manner. Since Richard was constantly on the road traveling, Lisa was often asked, "Where's Richard?" Aptly inspired by the popular hide-and-seek *Where's Waldo?* cartoon books, she decided Richard's whereabouts

{No Gifts Please}

For many people, the thought of having friends feel obligated to buy a present every time their birthday rolls around is enough to discourage them from having a party at all. Fortunately, there are many ways to use an invitation to politely discourage gift giving and to suggest more meaningful and creative alternatives.

A notation of "No gifts please" is the standard phrase, although there are certainly more clever ways to phrase it, such as "Your presence is the present." For those who prefer that a donation be made to a certain charity, it's customary to insert a card stating their request along with the charity's address and phone number and perhaps some background information about the services the charity provides.

A host can also encourage his guests to participate in an inspirational gift—a "living journal." The invitation explains that, in lieu of a gift, each guest should bring to the party a cherished memory about the celebrant. It could be in the form of a photograph, a poem, a drawing, or a special written recollection. One example was Bill Melamed's fortieth birthday. His invitation read, ". . . Don't even think about bringing me a gift. Instead, use the enclosed card to share a memory of our journey together in words, pictures, or whatever . . . and bring it with you." (Indeed, even those people who couldn't attend could take part in the activity.) Enclosed was a 9-by-12-inch heavily textured card that was blank save for the words along the bottom, ". . . and so the journey continues." When guests arrived at the party, they deposited their cards on a table at the entrance. They were undoubtedly cherished tributes that the host would keep for a lifetime.

...the ...dinner... ...iael's Restaurant... ...fabulous evening and I want you to be there. Wear Black Tie... Don't even think about bringing me a gift. Instead, use the enclosed card to share a memory... ...journey together... ...pictures, or whatever in ...r it with you.

Since Richard is no where to be found, word has it that in lieu of gifts, donations can be made in his honor to:

The Neil Bogart Memorial Fund
775 North Fairfax Road
...Hills, CA 90210

PRESENCE IS THE PRESENT

It's a sultry summer's night
of
Moroccan Feast & Fantasy

...join me for my birthday celeb...
...day, the...

A SULTRY MOROCCAN FETE,
complete with snake charmers and flame throwers to honor ballet
patron Patricia Kennedy on her fortieth birthday, was announced using
an invitation designed with drapes of vivid chiffons, a metallic-brocade
border, and a brass sunburst finding.

would be the theme of the outrageous surprise party held at Los Angeles's most famous train station, Union Station. To create the invitations, a very talented illustrator was on hand as Lisa talked about the key elements of Richard's life—their home life, family vacations in Hawaii, tennis games, and, of course, his job. The final result was a whimsical, elaborate pop-up card that not only encapsulated Richard's life and humor but became a gift in itself—to Richard and to his friends.

The use of photographs also makes a powerful statement for celebrants of any age. If the invitation features a portrait, make sure it represents a happy time, as would a winning childhood snapshot or a glamour pose from, say, the 1940s. Current pictures also work well as long as they are spirited and comfortable looking. Actually, the most ingenious use of photography results from some doctoring through modern computer technology. When Karen and Stan Winston were honoring their mutual fiftieth birthdays, they produced a composite photo of their baby photos, creating the illusion that they had been friends since birth, playing together in the same crib. Of course, it helped that Stan, the special effects wizard behind the movie *Jurassic Park* and others, did the computer imaging himself.

Although there are certainly no specific rules as to how a birthday should be commemorated, people approaching their golden years tend to favor simple elegance, particularly if the gathering is going to be a formal dinner party. Embroidered fabrics or silk moirés might serve as envelope liners, while papers in dark, rich tones such as Venetian red and teal, and silver or gold metallic inks, might make up the invitation. Invitations can be personalized by having the

KAREN AND STAN WINSTON'S mutual fiftieth birthday invitation, ABOVE, was made possible through the use of modern digital graphic technology. Their childhood photos were manipulated to give the appearance that their friendship began at birth. Combining clever copy (with phone R.S.V.P.s made to Ms. Liv Tu Party), an offbeat color palette, and a 3-D design of stripes, spirals, and spots, this invitation, BELOW, beckons friends to what promises to be a spirited evening.

S unday May 18th is the date-
whatever you do, please don't be late.
Arrive at 12 and stay till half past 2,
there will be lots of interesting things to do.
Your being there will be a joy to Melanie and me,
as I give this special party
with love, delight and glee !

Joan

X ♡ ♡ X X ♡

BRIGHTLY COLORED CARTOONS

in lime, tangerine, sun yellow, and bright blue were created for Melanie Borinstein's magical storytelling party adventure celebrating her fourth birthday, ABOVE. Frank Marshall's fiftieth birthday invitation, BELOW, filled with magic, music, and movies provided all of the inspiration necessary to make his boxed contraption literally leap from the page. Extra help was provided by an intricate rubber-band spring that ejected the invitation's information into the air.

guest's name calligraphed directly onto the card by leaving a space for it. The typeface should be clear and easy to read without being too fussy. A woman's birthday luncheon invitation can be equally elegant in its presentation while incorporating less austere touches, such as pastels, florals, or dried flowers.

For young children, it is important to keep in mind that the invitations should not be too "grown-up," and should reflect the child's age and personality. The most enchanting children's invitations have a whimsical, magical quality, be it contemporary or nostalgic. There's nothing more delightful than a storybook format—either as an unfolding accordion card or a format reminiscent of old-fashioned cloth-covered children's books. These small storybooks, covered with bright-colored printed fabrics and filled with hand-sewn pages, allow for a progressive narrative and provide a great opportunity for parents to get involved by crafting a tale about the child's personality, interests, or favorite stories. Just as with adults, this gives your child a sense of uniqueness far more than any store-bought card preprinted with the cartoon hero of the moment.

It's an evening of
MAGIC, MUSIC & MOVIES
in celebration of
Frank Marshall's
50th Birthday
October 4, 1996

Directions Enclosed

SUGAR RAY LEONARD'S

1970s image was spoofed, complete with a black velour Afro, in his disco-inspired fortieth-birthday bash invitation, which called for family and friends to arrive decked out in their finest polyester. The acid purple envelope, addressed in vibrant orange ink, was lined with the matching velour.

Enter the era
he doesn't let us forget...

Put away your fancy jewels
Pull out your plastic beads
Slide into your finest polyester
Get into the groove
and let's celebrate

RAY'S SURPRISE
40TH BIRTHDAY

Saturday, May 18

Sugar's Lounge

square
surprise

7:30 pm
Don't ev

[Queen B]

RSVP enclosed

ARMEN WEITZMAN,

together with his parents Margaret and Howard, merged their hip styles and contemporary sophistication in his Bar Mitzvah invitation. His name embossed in bold irregular type was the perfect complement for the op art–inspired forms infused with a blue and pea-green color combination.

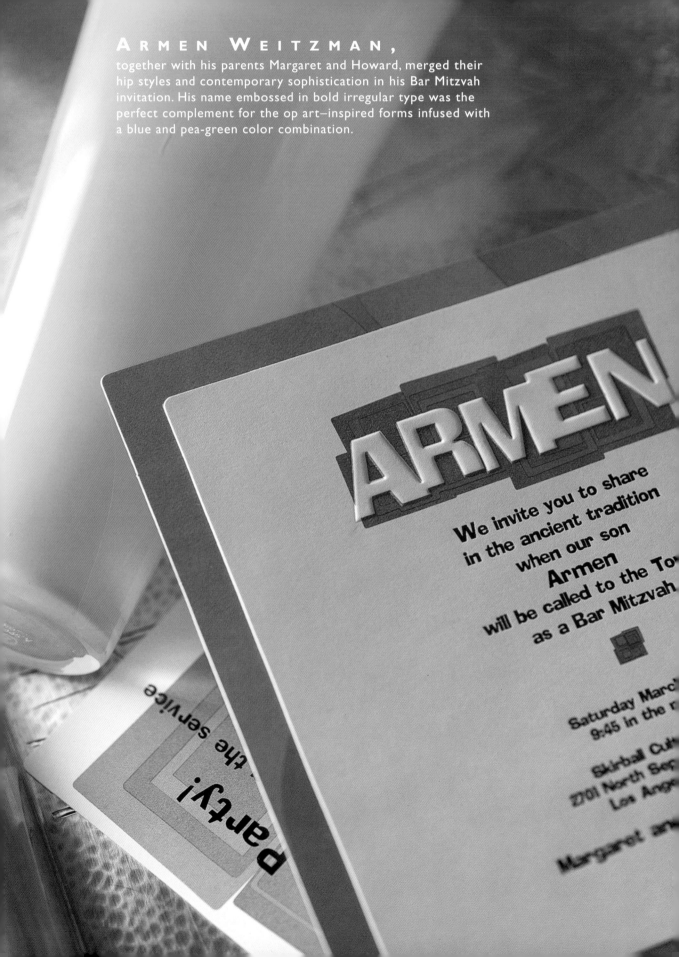

ARMEN

We invite you to share
in the ancient tradition
when our son
Armen
will be called to the To...
as a Bar Mitzvah

Saturday Marc...
9:45 in the m...

Skirball Cult...
2701 North Sep...
Los Ange...

Margaret an...

party!
...the service

RITES OF PASSAGE

4

LIFE'S JOY-FILLED turning points call for invitations with an inherent sense of honesty. These once-in-a-lifetime events honor personal accomplishments—whether they involve celebrating a renewed sense of love and commitment to a spouse or the achievement of earning a degree.

This form of expression often requires restraint, simplicity of design, and words from the heart. Complex constructions and unnecessary gimmicks only detract from the earnest, essential message. Sugarcoated sentimentality—as in the image of clinking champagne glasses and the not-too-subtle announcement, "It's our golden anniversary!"—not only trivializes the remarkable, but sets an impersonal tone.

THE BAPTISM & FIRST BIRTHDAY
invitation of Kenneth Valadez, son of Carolina Williams and
Arturo Valadez, featured a hand-tinted photograph of their
firstborn complete with angel's wings and a gold and navy,
celestial-inspired fabric lining the envelope.

GRADUATION INVITATIONS
reflect the personalities and interests of new graduates
Rebecca Bloom and Spencer Rascoff. Rebecca's, inspired by
her parents Ruth and Jake Bloom's passion for contemporary art, utilizes a colored self-portrait, printed on acetate,
fastened by metal eyelets to a bright orange stock. The
front of Spencer's vivid teal and orange invitations was a
photo collage of his friends and family.

When the rite of passage is religious, such as the
confirmation of a young adult or the Bar or Bat
Mitzvah of someone turning thirteen, the spiritual
nature of the event should dictate the choices of
design. Of course, the seriousness of the celebration
should not be confused with the formality reflected
in engraved wedding invitations. Since Bar and Bat
Mitzvahs coincide with a birthday, it is popular to
follow the religious ceremony with a theme-
oriented party. However, carrying these themes into
the invitation is not appropriate because it detracts
from the religious importance. Some people prefer
to send two separate invitations—a formal one for
the service and a playful one for the party.

The best invitations are inevitably a result of
involving a child in the design process. Since young
people are exposed to a broad visual vocabulary at
an early age—from computer graphics to television,
movies, and music videos—working with them on
the invitation is a way to nurture their own definitive style and to provide a sense of authorship.

One splendid example of this came from the
hand of Rebecca Hoffman, a Bat Mitzvah girl, who
drew a fantastic array of butterflies, the perfect symbol of transformation, for the design motif on her
invitation. The butterflies reappeared on the
decorative return address "plaque," which was also
used to seal the envelope.

When parents and their children have utterly different personal styles, a creative middle ground can
always be found. One challenging face-off occurred
when Bat Mitzvah girl Sara Rosen loved the heavy
metal group Guns N' Roses, while her mother, Rikki,
loved merely roses. Their inspired meeting of the
minds was a beautiful, crisp photograph of red roses
that became a stunning backdrop for the invitation.

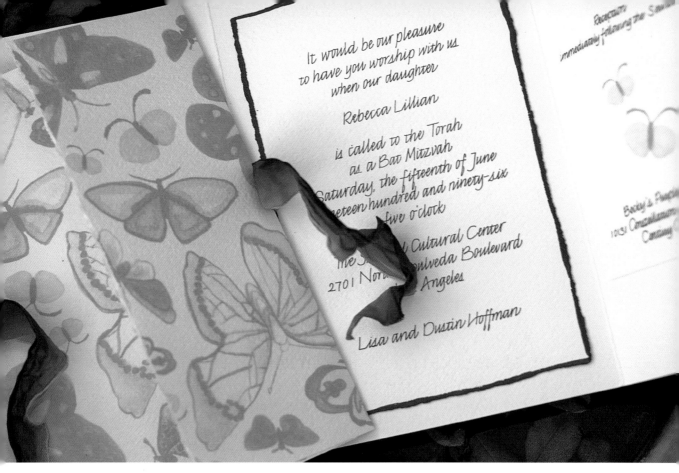

It would be our pleasure
to have you worship with us
when our daughter

Rebecca Lillian

is called to the Torah
as a Bat Mitzvah
Saturday, the fifteenth of June
nineteen hundred and ninety-six
five o'clock

the ... Cultural Center
2701 Nor... ...lveda Boulevard
... Angeles

Lisa and Dustin Hoffman

BEAUTIFUL BUTTERFLIES
hand-drawn by Bat Mitzvah girl Rebecca Hoffman formed the symbolic and poetic theme and backdrop to her invitation commemorating her meaningful and spiritual transition and rite of passage.

An overlay contained a choice verse from the group's hit song, "Sweet Child o' Mine." Sara's friends thought it was cool, and her grandparents, unaware of the lyrics' origin, simply cried.

Then there are the unusual role reversals where the children want a fancy invitation to portray their polish and cultural awareness while their parents prefer a low-key, casual style. One colorful compromise involved an artful ode to the 1960s: Armen Weitzman's Bar Mitzvah invitation merged op art and Rudi Gernreich–inspired shapes and colors with a playful, irregular typeface.

As people grow older, photographs unleash a flood of memories, especially when they are used for celebrations. A college-graduation photo montage, a sepia-toned wedding portrait, or even a contemporary picture of a couple surrounded by their clan, acknowledges the passage of time and affirms the stages of a life shared. When Ruth and Elliot Handler, creators of the Barbie doll and founders of Mattel Toys, gathered their friends for a party commemorating their mutual eightieth birthdays and fifty-eight years of marriage, a painting by Elliot of his wedding memories became the invitation's visual centerpiece.

Certainly the most difficult rite of passage to recognize is the death of a loved one. In much the same way a tribute acknowledges someone when he or she is savoring life's sweetest moments, memorial cards can

CELEBRATIONS

R U T H   A N D   E L L I O T   H A N D L E R ,
founders of Mattel and creators of Barbie and Hot Wheels, announced their fifty-eighth anniversary with an invitation incorporating the painting that Elliot gave his wife in honor of their momentous journey together. Roses and an excerpt from Sara Rosen's favorite song gave this invitation, OPPOSITE TOP, for the daughter of Rikki and Fred Rosen a dramatic impact. Screenwriter John Reis's striking portrait with his own words, OPPOSITE BOTTOM, graced his memorial announcement with reverence and intimacy—accentuated with an air of fragility through the use of the translucent overlay.

capture and honor someone's spirit when that person passes away. Whether the card serves as an invitation to the memorial service or as a handout at the tribute, it should be a testament to the individual's innermost self, his experiences, relationships, and the meaning of his life. On a practical level, the memorial card should indicate the full name of the deceased, the date of birth and death, the person officiating at the service, a list of speakers, and, if desired, a charity to which one can donate money.

Choosing which elements to include in a memorial card, such as a special photograph, favorite expressions, or passages from books or poems, can be an integral part of the healing process. By no means should the cards be morbid or depressing; they should symbolize the continuation of life. For example, nature is the perfect medium for inspiration. Blending elements such as leaves and flowers, organic papers, and soft inks can prove to be particularly poignant and beautiful.

Invitations should be mailed no less than three weeks before an event. Less than that and it's difficult to determine a final head count for a caterer or to begin working on seating arrangements. That means the invitations should not only be printed, but addressed, stamped, and ready to mail. It's always best to be early rather than late, so pad your schedule by an extra week or two in case there is a glitch at the printer or a federal holiday when the mailing is scheduled. Invitations for weddings and large fund-raisers should be sent at least six weeks before the event since so many details depend on the number of guests. If there are a lot of guests from out of state or out of the country, tack on another two weeks.

Working backward from an event date, some people start thinking about an invitation design a full year in advance. If that seems too much, consider starting at least six or seven months ahead. If time is of the essence, the printer should produce the envelopes first so they can be addressed and stamped while the rest of the order is being filled. On average, an experienced calligrapher can address fifteen envelopes per hour, but be sure to allow time to proof the addresses once they are done. And remember, if you're running late, rush charges may increase the cost as much as 50 percent.

A few important postal guidelines: Return addresses (commonly used without a name) should appear on the reverse side of an addressed and stamped envelope. To make sure that invitations arrive in the condition in which they were sent, a hand-canceling request noted on the lower left-hand corner will prevent envelopes from getting "tire tracks" from automated canceling equipment. This is particularly important for envelopes larger than $1/8$-inch thick or for those containing fragile materials. And always check with the post office for correct first-class postage.

Mrs. Sandra Pressman

and

Dr. and Mrs. Samuel Kunin

request the honor of your presence

at the marriage of

Nathalie Anne

Saturday, the tenth of

Nineteen hundred and

six forty-five o'clock in

Hillcrest Country

10000 West Pico

Los Ang

Black Tie

FRENCH VARIEGATED RIBBON
tied in a square Windsor knot and two-toned deckled edges make for an
elegant presentation of Sandy Pressman's wedding invitation for her daughter,
Nathalie Frankel, to Douglas Kunin.

MARRY ME

5

FROM THE DIAMOND that adorns the engagement ring to the bride's first slice into a towering white cake, weddings reflect centuries of custom. However, in the same way that an emerald ring and a deep, dark chocolate cake are acceptable wedding choices, invitation traditions can adapt to modern couples without sacrificing any of their significance.

Without a doubt, the most recognized wedding invitation format is a white or ecru, extra-thick, single-panel card or a medium-weight foldover. The type, always engraved in black ink, most often appears as a fancy, calligraphed copperplate script or as tailored, engraver's Roman block letters. Yet elegance comes in a wide spectrum. Deep, rich colors of ink, such as sapphire, cordovan, or dusty gold, impart a ceremonial touch. Paper with a beige-on-beige, ornamental-flourish

On Saturday, May 4, 1996
we experienced the most beautiful day of our lives
as we exchanged our wedding vows
upon the shores of Montego Bay, Jamaica
under the setting sun.

Keisha and Forest Whitaker

K EISHA AND F OREST W HITAKER
notified friends of their private Jamaican oceanfront ceremony with an announcement made from pale blue handmade paper embedded with seashells and a raffia bow affixed to a real starfish.

pattern and tied with a gold tassel provides an air of distinction. An oversize scroll printed in a scripted, storybook hand and emphasized with a gorgeous oversize initial cap creates an aura of fantasy.

New traditions of invitation styles also are emerging through colors, textures, and materials that suggest the inherent beauty of weddings held in natural settings. For a dinner at a posh Los Angeles beach club, one couple adorned their invitations with starfish affixed with ties of natural-colored net ribbon. For autumn nuptials taking place in the bride's family's winery set among the breathtaking vineyards of Larkspur, California, fat clusters of brass grapes graced the invitations like brooches. Off the coast of Seattle, Lopez Island's magnificent moss-covered rocks and forest inspired a garden wedding invitation; hand-marbled paper in shades of sage, taupe, and charcoal lined the envelopes and provided the backdrop for the printed cards.

Of course, one of the most rapidly changing time-honored conventions is to have the bride-to-be's parents give her away, pay for the wedding, and send out the invitations in their name. Since many couples now plan and give their own weddings—whether it's their first, second, or third—a new protocol with corresponding elements of style is growing in popularity. More and more, the bride and groom together help to design and select the invitation. These couples want to ensure that the final product reflects their combined tastes and sensibilities rather than conforming to someone else's dictates. This applies to young couples marrying for the first time who lean toward more fanciful invitations as well as to remarrying couples who desire understated simplicity.

No detail is small enough to overlook. A carefully chosen stamp for both the mailing envelope and the R.S.V.P. envelope is always noticed. "Love" stamps have now become wedding classics, with flowers and natural landscapes not far behind. Whenever possible, try to coordinate the color of the stamp with the colors of the paper, lining, or ink. If one stamp is insufficient, stamps of the same size and decorative value look more graceful, even if this requires some extra postage. An American flag isn't the right match for a gorgeous wildflower.

What the invitation says is as important as how it looks. Choosing the right words can be a daunting task for anyone who worries about appropriateness. There are many etiquette books on such matters that will answer sensitive questions, such as how to accommodate divorced parents (the rule is not to include the word "and" between their names) and how to correctly list the bride's mother when she is a medical doctor ("Mrs." is proper for social occasions). According to tradition, there are two long-held, standard wordings for the request line. "Mr. and Mrs. Leonard Klevan request the honour (note the spelling of honor) of your presence" has always been the norm for weddings in a house of worship. "Mr. and Mrs. Leonard Klevan request the pleasure of your company" is for wedding ceremonies taking place in all other locations.

Needless to say, depending on one's comfort level, the old, ironclad rules can adapt like everything else. A bride-to-be may simply decide to put her and her fiancé's first and last names at the bot-

COMBINING GOLD BEVELED EDGES
with rounded corners dressed with a loosely tied metallic gold tassel updates this traditional presentation while providing Allison Robbins and James Jennewain with the perfect invitation to their intimate, black tie New York wedding.

THE GARDEN WEDDING
of actress Lea Thompson to director Howard Deutsch was announced with an invitation printed in soft green and edged in metallic gold, sent in an envelope lined with beautiful abstract floral chintz.

i do.

On September 11, 1986 . . .
we made time for a date.

Eight years and nine months later,
he proposed . . .

by fax.

THE MODERN ROMANTIC ADVENTURE
of Liz Heller and John Manulis required nothing less than a witty invitation letterpressed on 100 percent cotton rag stock.

She accepted . . .
the next day . . .
by phone.

And now,
after nine years, three hundred and fifty-four days
and twenty two hours,
our adventure in modern romance continues . . .
in person.

tom of an invitation as if signing a letter. Or a couple may want to write their own message as an expression of their commitment to each other.

A couple should not be afraid to reflect warmth and passion, how they as a couple want to present themselves to the world, or even how they want their families represented. To accommodate a remarried mother-of-the-bride (who had kept her own name) as well as the groom's parents, invitations to a late-summer garden wedding were phrased, "Susan L. Taylor and Khephra Burns together with William Bowles invite you to celebrate with us the marriage of our daughter Shana Nequai to Bernard King, son of Thelma and Thomas King."

When a couple of the same sex want to ritualize their commitment to each other, the invitation's wording can follow the format of even the most traditional ones: "The pleasure of your company is requested at the commitment ceremony of Jeff Silverman and Ken Abby." Lighter in custom but not in meaning is this version: "Please join us at a get-together celebrating our getting together."

For couples who have a strong sense of humor, only a comical approach—or, perhaps, the absolute truth—will do. Elizabeth Heller, a record business executive, and John Manulis, a movie producer, devised clever copy about their high-powered,

invitation to their New Year's Eve fairy-tale wedding incorporated
a subtle mixture of tone on tone components that were tucked inside a
pocket inscribed with a romantic and moving
quotation by Pablo Neruda.

Ms. Connie Stevens
proudly requests the honour of your presence
at the celebration of the marriage of her daughter

Joely Fisher
to
Mr. Christopher Duddy

on New Year's Eve
Tuesday, the thirty-first of December
Nineteen hundred and ninety-six
promptly at six o'clock in the evening

IN MY SKY AT TWILIGHT YOU ARE LIKE A CLOUD AND YOUR FORM
AND COLOUR ARE THE WAY I LOVE THEM. YOU ARE MINE
AND IN YOUR LIFE MY INFINITE DREAMS LIVE

PABLO NERUDA

Sharon Lynn Summerall
and
Donald Hugh Henley

request the pleasure of your compa

at their wedding

...urday, the twentieth of...

...Nineteen hundred and ninety...

half past six o'clock

...P. Enclosed

...ets to follow

DON HENLEY AND SHARON SUMMERALL
invited guests to their breathtaking outdoor nuptials with a beautiful hand-embossed three-fold invitation that was closed with a wax seal embedded with a bronze angel. R.S.V.P. cards and reception inserts were held in place with a lush olive-green French-wired ribbon.

hectic lives that read: "On September 11, 1986 ... we made time for a date. Eight years and nine months later, he proposed ... by fax. She accepted ... the next day ... by phone. And now, after nine years, three hundred and fifty-four days and twenty-two hours, our adventure in modern romance continues ... in person." In another situation, nothing resembling hearts or flowers appeared on an offbeat yet elegant card; created from multiple fonts and icons, it included a TV antenna, a lightning bolt, and a most unusual message: "In our lifetime, the most impossible and unthinkable events have occurred ... Four lads from Liverpool changed the world, Man played golf on the moon, The remote control was invented. But now, the *most* impossible and unthinkable event is about to take place ... Darlene Chan and Frank De Palma are tying the knot!"

INSPIRED BY THE NATURAL BEAUTY of Lopez Island, off the coast of Seattle, Anne Willoughby and Nicholas Holt opted for a moss-green–scripted invitation bordered with a magnificent hand-marbled stone pattern of green, taupe, and black. The gold-deckled edge, wax seal, and French ribbon provided the finishing touches.

In addition to the actual wedding invitation, there are all manner of stationery and accessories that go along with getting married. From the bridal shower and the rehearsal dinner to itineraries describing pre- and postnuptial weekend activities, each event requires separate communication. Even though these are second to the wedding invitation, they all contribute to the grand vision of the perfect day and should be created accordingly.

Seated luncheons and sit-down dinners demand special accoutrements which can reflect the same visual vocabulary as the invitation. For instance, something as simple as a guest's name scrawled on a place card turns into a small keepsake when handwritten in calligraphy. The same paper, ink color, and design features can appear in escort cards, place cards, table numbers or names, and menus. A way to avoid using numbers comes from a couple who were married in the Caribbean. They chose symbols inspired by their setting—sun, fish, starfish, shells—written in the groom's native language of French. Using roman numerals or writing out the numbers are other alternatives. Foldover cards or numbers inserted into small picture frames provide an elegant tablescape as well.

To help avoid table clutter, individual menus work best when they are approximately 5 by 8 inches and fit on top of the service plate. The menu can also function as a place card when the guest's name is on top. Table favors can double as place cards, such as a slightly fragrant candle wrapped with a beautiful gold mesh ribbon, or boxed chocolate truffles with the guest's name written on a gift card.

Order thank-you notes at the same time as the invitations, since gifts arrive early. Many couples like to carry through the stylistic imagery of the invitation, which provides a visual consistency and allows the experience to continue after the wedding. Consider creating two versions, one with the bride's name for her shower gifts and one with the names of the bride and groom once they are married. When the bride keeps her own surname, first names can be used instead.

Now that many couples choose to have private ceremonies, wedding announcements are increasingly popular. Announcements require as much thought as an invitation in order to convey the combined spirit of the couple's relationship. Keisha and Forest Whitaker's announcement was set against a backdrop of handmade paper with shells, seaweed, and a starfish mounted on top, which reflected their Jamaican nuptials. The wording can also come from both sets of parents who are "pleased to announce the marriage of" their children. Or the announcement can be lighthearted and casual. Take, for example, Lloyd Cotsen and Margit Sperling, who sent friends a notice of their Aspen, Colorado, nuptials, suitably topped with an aspen leaf, which read in part, "As of September 17 Margit has a new last name. Lloyd has a big new smile."

PLACE CARD

Your presence here tonight
means so very much to us both!

Thank you for joining us in celebration!

Pamela and Steven
August 23, 1997

SAVE THE DATE

if the first glance from the face of the
beloved is like a seed sown & love in the field of
the heart, and the first flower on the branch of
lips is like the first kiss from two
the union is the first fruit of
that seed sown upon the record
please join us for much fruit!

save
NEW YE...

THANK YOU

Anne
&
Nick

TABLE NUMBERS

3

Hope your summer
is a moving experience...

PLEASE HANDLE
FRAGILE
THANK YOU
★ ★ ★

RUSH

PACKAGING STICKERS, TWINE,
and bubble wrap, the essential elements of any move, transformed
Michele and Michael Bernstein's simply printed moving announcement
into a memorable keepsake.

THE HOME FRONT

6

WHETHER HOME IS a downtown loft, a ten-acre ranch, or a modest bungalow, stationery for the home speaks volumes about personal taste and is extremely gratifying to send and receive. It can be used on the occasion of buying a first abode, finally completing a long overdue remodeling project, or hosting an at-home party for the benefit committee of an art museum gala.

People usually first consider integrating hearth and home into an expression on paper when they invite friends to a housewarming party or send out moving announcements. Moving to a new home marks the beginning of another chapter in life, especially when changing cities. It provides an opportune moment to make a statement about your new environment and to reconnect with long-lost friends.

for these at-home cards and correspondence notes is a creative combination of the first letters of partners Jonathan Canno and Jay Daggenhart's first names.

SUMPTUOUS MENUS

for photographer Greg Gorman's "Dom Perignon Dinner" were multilayered and tied with a French ribbon. Each guest's name was calligraphed on a paper band that wrapped around each menu (not shown) and doubled as a place card as well.

Something as simple as attaching a green plastic Monopoly-style house to a sturdy white card and adding one's name, new address, and phone number is a charming and direct way to broadcast the news of a move or to summon friends over for a first look. (A slightly oversized envelope will accommodate the raised piece along with a request for hand-canceling.) Even basic packaging materials can amusingly disseminate the news of a move. Upon their arrival in Malibu, staunch New Yorkers Michele and Michael Bernstein and their children informed friends about their new residence by wrapping a moving card inside bubble wrap and brown kraft paper, complete with FRAGILE and RUSH stickers. The "moving packages" were tied with twine and mailed in clear plastic envelopes that were sealed with standard-issue, red-bordered mailing labels. The final California touch was affixing return address labels decorated with palm trees.

Architecture also works as an influential design feature, whether with a simple sketch of a house's facade or with more intricate details. When Manhattan attorneys Bari Mattes and Michael O'Brien moved into their brilliantly designed and very contemporary loft space, an abstract and graphic interpretation of the architect's floor plan embellished the announcements. A paper-thin cherry-wood veneer, the same wood that appears throughout their house, ran along one side of the card with brushed-aluminum embossed accents. The Mattes-O'Briens liked their announcements so much that they repeated the floor-plan image in their housewarming party invitations, place cards for their first sit-down dinner, and stationery for their home.

No new home is complete without its own stationery. As an alternative to monogrammed corre-

MODERN ARCHITECTURAL ELEMENTS

provided the graphic inspiration for the housewarming announcements and personalized stationery of New York attorneys and consummate entertainers Bari Mattes and Michael O'Brien, whose downtown loft is fashioned from curved stainless steel and cherry. The type was printed in pearlized champagne foil.

spondences or personalized note cards, household stationery reflects the uniqueness of a home and acts as a window to another part of your life, particularly if your letter writing is done mostly on business stationery. Made from heavyweight card stock and measuring approximately 4 by 6 inches (and designed to be used either horizontally or vertically), house stationery is great for dashing off a quick note, for gift enclosures, or for handwritten invitations to informal at-home parties given on short notice. Visiting houseguests also will appreciate having stationery available for their own correspondence. Prominently display the stationery on top of a desk or table in a beautiful leather paper holder, in a wood or velvet-covered box, or in an antique silver toast rack. Another way to use house stationery is to reproduce the chosen image on a memo pad kept near the telephone.

Traditionally, an engraved pineapple, the symbol of hospitality, and other images from nature—the Napoleonic bee, a rose, a seashell—have embellished informal note cards. Instead, along with your address, you can feature the name of your house (or come up with one if you haven't already), a beloved tree from your garden, a statue, or a detail such as a column, window, or the front door. Creative Intelligence managing director Dan Nadeau and his partner, D. J. Peterson, display the directions to their house, artistically written

*It is said that the spring evening air
holds the notes and the songs just a moment longer.
For this reason we cordially invite you to join us
at our home
for an evening with
the Los Angeles Opera Company*

Saturday, March 23
in the evening
Road

Arthur and Lauren Levine

A POETIC VERSE
and a beautiful bronze cherub set the tone for Los
Angeles Opera patrons Lauren Leichtman and Arthur
Levine's magical, musical, entertaining evening at home.

and then letterpressed onto stationery. Another symbol of the home that adds a warm, personal touch to any card is a picture of a pet. For that matter, create stationery reserved expressly for one of your animals to use when gifts come their way. Naturally, my own dog is outfitted with her very own notes that read: "From the doghouse of Luvee."

The possibilities for invitations to parties held at home are as plentiful as the types of festivities. In its own sort of shorthand, the invitation should spell out the tone of the event, let guests know exactly what to expect when they arrive, tell them how they should dress, if they need to appear precisely at the strike of the hour, whether they should bring a gift, and also, perhaps, the kind of food they'll be eating—a Moroccan feast or hotdogs with corn on the cob.

For casual meals, it's best to avoid fuss, fancy papers, and elaborate calligraphy. An appropriate card would be the host's handwriting on a beautifully colored paper, perhaps accented with the colors of the season, the linens you're using, or the shade of your dining room walls. Free-form printing and using all lowercase letters also add an air of informality. For an easygoing get-together, wording should follow suit: "Come over for an evening of friends and food." You can invent your own instructions for attire, such as, "Dress: Up!" or "Please wear something." The time called for can be "eight-ish" rather than eight o'clock sharp. Bill Melamed, with his remarkable knack for throwing great birthday bashes, came up with one of my all-time favorite expressions for gift giving: "Lavish gifts optional." For groups smaller than twenty, a phone R.S.V.P. request in the lower left-hand corner is perfectly appropriate.

Holiday parties usually call for extra effort on all fronts. To entice guests to a Valentine's Day dinner,

{ PAPER FAVORS }

The perfect favor completes the perfect party. It is true that everyone loves receiving a gift, but a memento that evokes a person or event is particularly special. For that reason, party favors belong in their own special class—they create a lasting impression of a special celebration and act as a memorable and sometimes practical present. Of course, any favor involving paper and writing is ideal.

When beautifully calligraphed, place cards become a souvenir. For one party, the place cards were elaborate sculptural constructions of heavy paper and metal, each one slightly different and all truly works of art, which everyone took home. Menus or programs can act in the same manner, especially if they are handmade or include unique accents.

If you have the time to plan far ahead, personalized stationery makes your guests feel that you truly appreciated their presence because you went to the trouble of creating such a thoughtful gift. Of course, personalizing stationery means knowing exactly who will attend, and it is always smart to order extra plain cards, just in case of last-minute changes. The stationery, when tied in a bow, also can be a substitute for place cards.

Various kinds of boxes can make elegant favors as well. Handmade boxes made from beautiful papers can be filled with plain note cards in a matching paper. A small hand-painted wooden box can hold brilliantly colored flowers along with a set of notes made from organic paper and embedded with wildflower petals.

Exquisite glass-tipped dipping pens can accompany a handsome bottle of imported ink. Or give each guest a seal with his or her last initial tied to a set of sealing-wax candles.

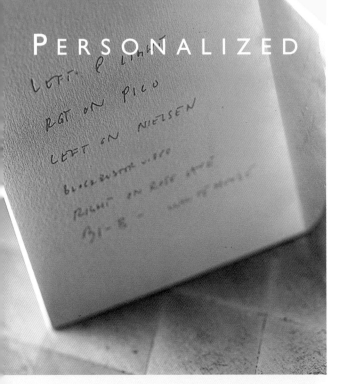

TRAVEL DIRECTIONS

were the unusual inspiration for these taupe, letterpressed, whimsical note cards, ABOVE, given by Dan Nadeau to his partner on their first anniversary. My dog, Luvee, is outfitted with tasteful stationery, BELOW, direct from her dog house, signed of course with her pawprint.

Rikki and Fred Rosen sent heart-shaped brocade boxes filled with antique rose potpourri. The actual invitation, handwritten on a beautiful cotton rag paper edged in garnet and gold, resembled an antique Victorian valentine. As an added special gesture, they were hand-delivered. Scott Sanders announced a Fourth of July celebration at his beachfront house in Amagansett, Long Island, using a five-panel accordion-folded card with bold patterns of patriotic colors, old-world firecrackers, a graphically enhanced portrait of the Statue of Liberty, and the edict: "Come party! Express your independence!"

At proper sit-down lunches and dinners, place cards and menus are undoubtedly elegant touches, but they also serve a practical purpose. Place cards remove the awkwardness of not knowing where to sit, and menus allow guests the pleasure of savoring the delicacies to come. Both can consist of very simple calligraphy on standard, off-white card stock, or they can relate directly to the style or theme of the event. When the Los Angeles County Museum of Art asked various collectors around town to simultaneously host dinners in their homes for museum supporters, Joan Borinstein, philanthropist and consummate hostess, set small easels at each person's place. Each of the courses had been inspired by a different work of art in her collection. The easels presented each course on individual cards along with the image of the corresponding painting.

When home entertaining includes dignitaries or heads of state, table accessories can, in their own quiet way, help commemorate an event. Hosting a

OLD-WORLD ENGRAVINGS

depicting costumes from a Venetian Carnivale were letterpressed in rich, jewel-toned pigments and bordered with a hand-tooled embossed border on deckled-edge cotton rag. Packaged with a hand-blown glass dip pen and ink, the set served as a great favor for guests attending a masquerade ball.

White House Endowment Fund dinner where First Lady Hillary Clinton was the guest of honor, Universal Studios chairman and chief executive officer Frank Biondi and his wife, Carol, attended to every detail. The White House facade, embossed in gold, not only appeared on the menus, which doubled as place cards, and on the table seating cards, but also on the napkins and even the hand towels for the bathroom.

PERSONALITY

HARK!

AN ANGELIC ILLUSTRATION
drawn on the computer by Anne Costner, daughter of Cindy and
Kevin Costner, is combined with bold direct text and captures the
innocence of the holiday season.

A SEASON OF ORIGINALITY

7

IT WOULDN'T BE THE HOLIDAYS without an avalanche of cards in the mailbox. Somehow, certain ones stand out from the pile and find a prized place on the fireplace mantel. And long after the gifts are unwrapped and the lights are turned off, many people remember their favorites. Stored in a shoebox or a miscellaneous drawer, holiday cards bring warm thoughts and joyous memories year after year, much like pages in a cherished scrapbook.

Whether the message is spiritual, whimsical, or imaginative, holiday greetings touch people's hearts and souls. The sentiment can be familiar and perhaps contained in just a few choice words, such as "Cheers," "Peace," "Rejoice," or "Merry Everything." But it is the design, use of materials, processes, and type styles that set the message apart. There is no better example of the medium transforming

In the spirit of the Holiday Season
a donation has been made
in your name to

e AIDS Memorial G

memorial located in Gold
·o hope, healing, and

A REAL LEAF
attached with raffia reflects the natural beauty of The
National AIDS Memorial Grove, a living memorial located
in Golden Gate Park, the beneficiary of this holiday greeting sent by entertainment agent Scott Arnovitz.

THE INTRICATE IRONWORK
pattern from Kenny G and his wife Lyndie's new home
provided the template for the die-cut and embossed gatefold holiday greeting that also notified friends and family
about their recent move.

the message as with a truly inspired holiday card.

Rarely are the most memorable cards the ones of the store-bought variety. In fact, there's nothing more disappointing than opening an envelope to find a card identical to one that someone else already sent. But with a little thought and moderate organization, anyone can create holiday cards well before the winter rush. Because the holidays conjure up a wide range of powerful emotions firmly rooted in a person's ethnic tradition, religious beliefs, and family history, expressing those feelings can be an exhilarating process with meaningful results for those who send them. And the yearly ritual of creating holiday missives can become a seasonal custom, like baking Christmas cookies or lighting Hanukkah candles.

The most traditional holiday cards celebrate Christmas, Hanukkah, and the New Year, but there are many other possibilities. An interfaith couple may want to send greetings representing both of their religions. One couple chose a whimsical contemporary illustration of a Santa Claus approaching a house with a Christmas tree and a Hanukkah menorah in the window. Santa is standing near the door with his hands on his hips, looking confused and saying, "Oy." Inside, the greeting reads, "Jingle all the vey."

An increasingly popular approach is a secular, nondenominational card that celebrates the global aspirations of sharing, unity, or peace, or simply gives thanks for the completion of the year with a look toward the next. Universal symbols containing diverse cultural images—old-world musical instruments, doves, stars, children, cherubs, or winter accents such as acorns or evergreen sprigs—suit several themes and evoke heartfelt sentiments.

Since etiquette rules for holiday cards are not as stringent as they are for wedding announcements

a New York literary agency known for its eclectic clientele, shared a burst of holiday cheer with their classic column corporate logo blind-embossed and topped with a bright red star and golden starburst. "Peace and Merry Everything" stated the agency's sentiment directly and to the point.

PEACE
and
MERRY
EVERYTHING

To have enough to share -
to know the joy of giving;
To thrill with all the sweets of life -
is living.

or party invitations, celebrating the season is an ideal opportunity to be expressive and creative. Someone may want to be gloriously festive by using materials such as rich jewel-toned papers, bas-relief metallic adornments, and multicolored silk or iridescent wired ribbons. Another person may prefer handcrafted papers combined with elements of nature, such as pressed leaves or bits of twig, to reflect a low-key, austere sensibility that honors the gifts of the earth.

Experimenting with color helps to avoid overused imagery. A combination of unusual shades, such as chocolate brown, burgundy, cranberry, and lime, can replace the familiar bright reds and greens of Christmas. Or consider subtle earth tones like olive green and coppery rust, or jewel tones such as emerald, sapphire, and amethyst, which add a richness to cards. Bright whites and silver can invoke a virgin snowfall, while natural whites with golden highlights communicate ethereal messages of spiritual purity. Gold or another metallic shade, even when used sparingly, adds a touch of regalness and a feeling of importance, as well as a bit of sparkle. Artful papers and fabrics, including beautiful Italian marbled stationery, pearlescent embossed floral cards, or fabrics woven from luminescent threads, can provide an unexpected backdrop for any message.

If using conventional holiday images, they should have artistic merit, such as reproductions of old Currier

filled with
HARMONY & GRACE

{A SEASON OF GIVING}

More and more people are opting to use their holiday greeting cards in a socially responsible manner. There is a heightened awareness of social, cultural, and medical needs and a backlash against the excesses and commercialism of the holiday season. When people opt not to give gifts to the many people in their lives and instead to donate money in their honor, their generosity can appear in several ways.

Insert cards, sometimes made of vellum, give the contribution a sense of importance and can include the charity's mission statement. A gift can also be indicated on one panel of a one- or two-panel fold-over card; it can appear underneath the giver's name, or it can be incorporated into the main message.

People who cannot choose between their favorite charities and give to more than one can list them all on the card. In fact, giving doesn't even have to wait until Christmas or Hanukkah. Sometimes people send out such cards for Thanksgiving, which becomes a way to start the holiday season off in a warm, compassionate, and thankful way.

Corporate holiday cards follow much the same guidelines as personal ones, although companies with many different locations may choose to tailor their giving to charities located in various regions. One year, the Los Angeles law firm Alschuler, Grossman & Pines sent cards in the form of deep green legal file folders written in legalese and labeled "Case No. 1996." "In the Spirit of Giving, we hereby stipulate and agree to make a substantial contribution in your honor to The Fulfillment Fund, a mentoring and scholarship program for... disadvantaged students."

& Ives–styled engravings or classic winter landscapes. Less common but equally suitable, contemporary or abstract interpretations of traditional symbols can also make a strong impact. Ruth and Jake Bloom, a Los Angeles art dealer and her prominent attorney husband, sent invitations for their annual Hanukkah open house with images of candles created from strips of bamboo and lit with flames made of brass sheet metal. Artist Hiro Yamagata used a photograph from one of his recent exhibitions—the front end of a restored and painted 1930s Mercedes—as the cover of a holiday card. The sensational photograph was matched by the wit of the inscription, which read, "Merry Christmas, Happy New Year, Happy Hanukkah, Happy Easter, Happy Buddha, Happy Thanksgiving, Happy Valentine's Day & Happy Birthday to You!"

Since the holidays are celebrations for the whole family, a child's illustration, whether reproduced from a drawing or taken from the computer, can earn a prime position on a card's cover. The child's involvement in the creation of the image not only imparts a sweet sense of innocence and guarantees a one-of-a-kind creation, but provides a sense of pride and value if the "artist" gets acknowledged on the back of the card.

The long-standing tradition of using family photographs in holiday greetings does not mean the image has to look standard or boring. The style and manner in which the picture is taken, as well as the film type and printing process, can dramatically alter its look. Warm-toned black-and-white photographs printed on matte stock, or subtle, hand-tinted ones, have a classic feeling and adapt to unusual papers and colors better than regular film.

CASE NO. 1996

THE HOLIDAY MESSAGE
CONTAINED IN THIS FILE
IS PRIVILEGED

FOR YOUR EYES ONLY   FOR YOUR EYES ONLY

ALSCHULER, GROSSMAN & PINES

IN RE HAPPY HOLIDAYS,
a firm commitment.

CASE NO.
STIPULATION
(UNDER SEAL)

STIPULATION

In the Spirit of Giving, we hereby
stipulate and agree to make a
substantial contribution in your honor
to **The Fulfillment Fund**, a mentoring
scholarship program for high potential
but economically disadvantaged students
in the greater Los Angeles area.

Our Very Best Wishes For The New

STIPULATED AND AGREE

ALSCHULER, GROSSMAN

A LEGAL DOCUMENT
issued from the law firm of Alschuler, Grossman & Pines that
stipulated that their clients have a happy holiday. The authentic-
looking hunter-green folder was embellished with gold foil type.

We ask ourselves, who am I to be brilliant, gorgeous, talented and fabulous?

QUINCY JONES AND HIS FAMILY

gather every year to pose for their striking portrait that graces their holiday greeting. The photograph was inset into a bronze-embossed border on a rustic, recycled copper-toned card stock.

Stiff family portraits in which everyone wears matching red and green regalia express little holiday cheer. Some of the best shots are taken outside with natural light. The photograph may not even need to revolve around holiday themes. Pictures of children playing under the covers or running down a flight of stairs capture a fun, festive spirit without using any of the same old holiday clichés. Frank and Carol Biondi favored a simple snapshot of their two grown daughters relaxing at the beach with the family dog.

Since gathering family members for a photograph is increasingly difficult, especially when relatives are spread across the country and beyond, holiday celebrations are opportune times to seize the moment for a picture. On one such occasion, Quincy Jones and his large extended family opted for a hip, casual shot of them all leaning against a concrete wall. The image was mounted on a card and made a suitable holiday greeting. When families cannot assemble, photomontages can show bits of everyone's life and capsule the year, but, of course, photographs don't need to be limited to relatives.

When the holidays coincide with important life transitions, such as a move to a new house or the birth of a child, both events can be marked at the same time. A New York couple who had recently made Los Angeles their second home adorned their cards with an ornament-trimmed palm tree and the message: "Wishing you a happy holiday from the left coast." Producer Bud Yorkin and his wife, actress Cynthia Sykes, announced the arrival of their newborn daughter with holiday cards showing her picture bordered with holly. "We send you our bundle of joy along with best wishes for a wonderful holiday season," read the card. It looked like a gift, wrapped in sheer tissue and tied with a Victorian wired ribbon of variegated shades of dusty rose. Clearly, it expressed their exuberance that the holiday had provided the best gift of all—their first child together.

Even businesses and corporations have a chance to exercise creative license when producing company holiday cards. If it is done correctly, with thought and imagination, companies can successfully demonstrate their appreciation for clients and customers. At the same time, a card can highlight a company's philanthropy if the card announces that a donation has been made to a charity in lieu of a gift.

Dressing up a company logo is yet another way businesses can deliver their holiday sentiments. Elephant Walk Entertainment once used embossed cards with their company's logo and mascot, a stately elephant, adorned with a robe of deep purple and gold jewels. If corporate logos are merely type styles, favorite quotes or images related to the nature of the business are also suitable. For his company's cards, Quincy Jones took inspiration from a quotation by one of Jones's musical heroes, Duke Ellington. A striking black-and-white photograph of Ellington sitting alone at his piano illuminated by a single ray of light provided the dramatic backdrop for the composer's poignant and moving words: "Every time God's children have thrown away fear in pursuit of honesty—trying to communicate, understood or not—miracles have happened." It was signed simply, "Peace & Unity, Quincy Jones Productions."

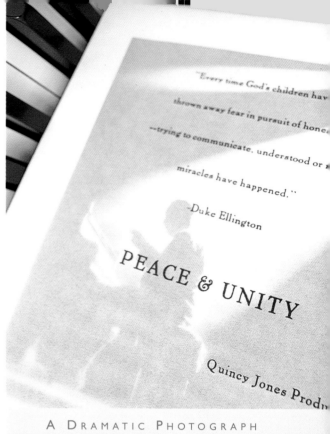

A DRAMATIC PHOTOGRAPH of Duke Ellington coupled with his moving quotation, ABOVE, captures the spirit and essence of Quincy Jones's music production company. A compelling black-and-white portrait of a child, BELOW, was the focal point for Ticketmaster Corporation's combined holiday greeting and charitable donation card.

the famed Italian jeweler, chose Steven Spielberg's Starbright Foundation as the beneficiary for this glamorous evening of jewels. The event celebrated the company's love for the glamour of Hollywood and the publication of a book on the origins of the Bvlgari style.

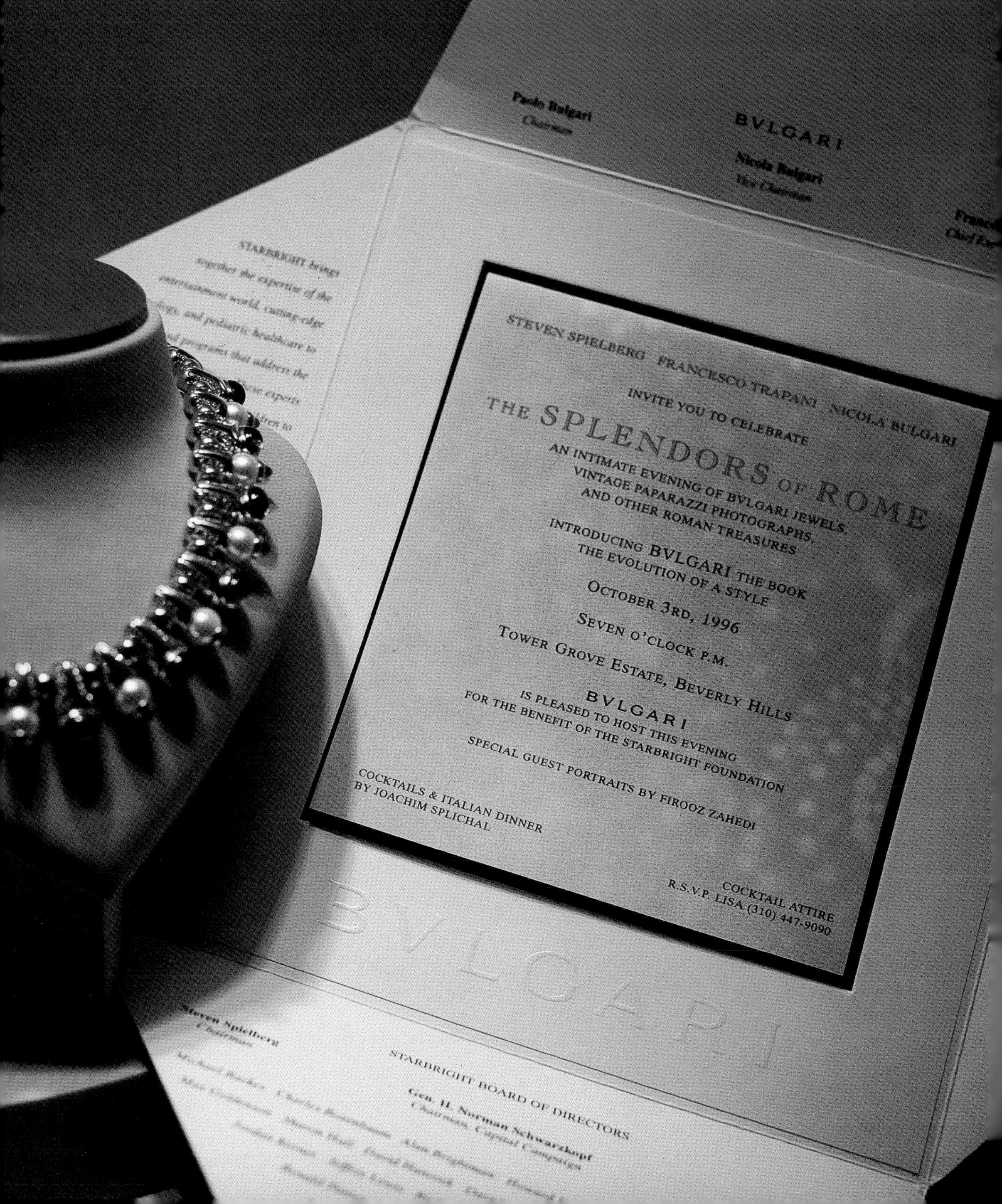

Paolo Bulgari
Chairman

BVLGARI

Nicola Bulgari
Vice Chairman

Franc
Chief Exe

STARBRIGHT brings together the expertise of the entertainment world, cutting-edge ology, and pediatric healthcare to al programs that address the ese experts dren to

STEVEN SPIELBERG   FRANCESCO TRAPANI   NICOLA BULGARI

INVITE YOU TO CELEBRATE

THE SPLENDORS OF ROME

AN INTIMATE EVENING OF BVLGARI JEWELS,
VINTAGE PAPARAZZI PHOTOGRAPHS,
AND OTHER ROMAN TREASURES

INTRODUCING BVLGARI THE BOOK
THE EVOLUTION OF A STYLE

OCTOBER 3RD, 1996

SEVEN O'CLOCK P.M.

TOWER GROVE ESTATE, BEVERLY HILLS

BVLGARI
IS PLEASED TO HOST THIS EVENING
FOR THE BENEFIT OF THE STARBRIGHT FOUNDATION

SPECIAL GUEST PORTRAITS BY FIROOZ ZAHEDI

COCKTAILS & ITALIAN DINNER
BY JOACHIM SPLICHAL

COCKTAIL ATTIRE
R.S.V.P. LISA (310) 447-9090

BVLGARI

Steven Spielberg
Chairman

STARBRIGHT BOARD OF DIRECTORS

Gen. H. Norman Schwarzkopf
Chairman, Capital Campaign

GALAS AND GREAT BIG BASHES

8

BUSINESS, CHARITABLE ORGANIZATIONS, and party-loving individuals all throw big bashes. Whether "big" means two hundred people or a cast of thousands, large-scale entertaining takes on a life of its own.

To attract a crowd, it's fair to say that invitations are the purest form of direct-mail marketing. Every successful event needs "buzz," that intangible, word-of-mouth energy that gets people talking, and the invitation is the definitive way to get it started. Invitations must grab the recipients' attention, involve them, and, of course, convince them that they must attend the function. Even when someone declines, there's still inherent value in an invitation that raises awareness or simply provides a conversation piece. Many people are reluctant to throw out something special and eye-catching. While one person may keep an invitation on top of his

or her desk, another may position it on a quilted memory board. Somewhere, the receiver's consciousness registers the hosting organization or individual inviting them to the fete.

From a planning perspective, the design and creation of an invitation influences almost every aspect of the party experience. It helps to establish "branding," the process (on which corporate America spends billions of dollars) that goes into giving a new product, service, or business a distinctive and unmistakable identity. The visual vocabulary that comes from brainstorming sessions with event planners—either the charity's gala committee or a company's marketing department—will influence all the components of an event, from its concept to menu selection, entertainment, and decor.

That's why it is so important, once the logistics

"FORBIDDEN PARADISE"

was the theme of a bash for Los Angeles's Museum of Contemporary Art young support group. The museum's logo appeared to be carved from the die-cut apple that unfolded to expose a venomous snake. Through the combination of color, typeface, and construction, the invitation provided a taste of the pleasures that could be expected at this ultrahip evening.

of GIVING

are determined, for the invitation to be next in line. Many companies or charities start mapping out party arrangements well over a year in advance, if not longer. It is at that point of inception when discussions about invitation design and event branding should take place. Because visual consistency is so important, any related material, such as programs and ad journals, should continue the invitation-inspired imagery and ideas. This too should happen in the earliest stage of an event's conception.

{CHARITY EVENTS}

Invitations for nonprofit institutions have their own inherent challenges. Almost all of them carry the primary purpose of raising money. Invitations should not appear as if they came directly from Madison Avenue, and they should not be grossly oversized or fashioned from pricey papers and processes, such as multiple-color engraving. At the same time, there is a subtle correlation between ticket price and the look of the invitation.

A community festival that charges $25 at the gate certainly should not send out anything luxurious looking, and invitations to a $1,000-per-plate dinner should not appear as if they were reproduced on a black-and-white photocopy machine. Keep in mind that the response rate for charitable functions can range from 10 to 15 percent, and prepare to print a quantity that meets your desired attendance goals. And, in order to keep costs low, the weight of the invitation, including inserts, should not exceed two ounces.

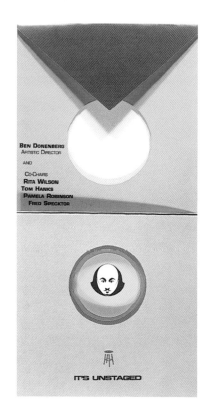

BEN DONENBERG
Artistic Director

AND

Co-Chairs
RITA WILSON
TOM HANKS
PAMELA ROBINSON
FRED SPECKTOR

IT'S UNSTAGED

"SIMPLY SHAKESPEARE,"
a celebrity reading of some of Will's greatest works bene-fiting Shakespeare Festival/LA, garnered record attendance with a new take on a familiar face, ABOVE. "Unveiling the Masterpiece," BELOW, was the theme of the festivities celebrating the expansion of the Santa Barbara Museum of Art's new building. A finely engraved ornate gilded frame was perfectly suited for the black tie gala.

SANTA BARBARA
MUSEUM OF
ART
UNVEILING THE MASTERPIECE

Many hosts attempt to be clever about requesting certain attire. But often they can confuse their guests. Suggestions like "Dress: Elegant," "Creative black tie," and "Black tie optional" can leave a person debating what is appropriate. Without taking away from the fun of guests dressing creatively, be very specific when the dress code is an integral part of the event.

The most frequently used dress-code suggestions are "cocktail attire"—suits for men and cocktail dresses or their equivalent for women—and "business attire." Slightly less dressy than cocktail attire, "business attire" means anything that is appropriate for the office, and it is customarily used for events held at the close of the business day. "Black tie" or "formal" indicate that men should wear tuxedos and women should wear either evening trousers or a ball gown, depending on what is customary. Rarely seen these days is "white tie," meaning white bow ties and tails for men and gowns for women, which summons up images of the splendor and elegance of a bygone era.

When a party is held outdoors or in a location that would make the usual party gear unsuitable, dress-code recommendations can be crucial to a guest's personal comfort. For a "Full Moon Garden Party" reception celebrating the marriage of Giorgio perfume cocreator Fred Hayman to his longtime love Betty Endo, the hosts were concerned that guests be forewarned about the dampness and cold that creep in when the sun sets at their ocean-front Malibu estate. The invitation stated black tie for men and, for ladies, "outdoor cocktail attire, shoes for lawn and evening wrap suggested."

As with all invitations, those for fund-raisers should reflect the personality of the organization and its constituents. The MOCA Contemporaries, a support group of the Museum of Contemporary Art in Los Angeles, draws its fund-raising dollars from many emerging philanthropists under the age of forty. Their invitations are highly conceptual, visually explosive, and hard-edged and transmit an urban sensibility. The Los Angeles Opera, with an older, more sophisticated audience, requires invitations that reflect the timeless elegance and grandeur of some of the world's greatest operatic masterpieces. Ecru cards with rounded corners, beveled edges, and beautiful scripts are indispensable. For the opening of *Fedora*, starring Placido Domingo and Maria Ewing, the costumer's sketches of the performance appeared on a watercolor-washed, translucent vellum that gracefully wrapped the main invitation. A diamond-shaped seal imprinted with a nineteenth-century engraving of a pair of ladies' shoes provided the finishing touch and secured the contents of the packet.

When galas have themes based on a specific time period, the best sources for imagery come from materials unearthed at the library, rare book stores, and flea markets. Photographs, illustrations, typefaces, and buzz words descriptive of a particular era make an inspiring source. For the ultimate disco extravaganza, the Los Angeles Center for Early Education based their invitation on the forbidding, roped-off doors and the obligatory red-carpeted entrance (imitated in red velour) of hot clubs like Studio 54. The gatefold "doors" opened to reveal that disco-era icon—the revolving mirrored ball (a three-dimensional mosaic foiled circle). A gold cord, like the ones that separated the "in" from the "out" crowd, provided the closure for the card.

A M E L I A   E A R H A R T ' S
flight log was the inspiration behind this old-fashioned journal-style invitation to the world premiere of the Turner Network Television's original movie.

A   T H R E E - D I M E N S I O N A L
television set designed with polka dots, stripes, and retro colors brought back memories of Mike, Dinah, and Merv for the Neil Bogart Memorial Fund's "TV Dinner" fund-raising event.

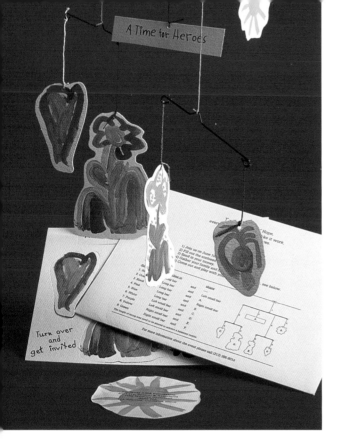

THE ELIZABETH GLASER PEDIATRIC AIDS FOUNDATION

salutes children living with AIDS at their annual "A Time for Heroes" fund-raising carnival. Corporate underwriting enabled the production of these whimsical invitations in the form of mobiles, ABOVE. The National AIDS Memorial Grove incorporated a haunting, hand-tinted photo, BELOW, to capture the right mood for "Twilight in the Grove," their first event in the Grove.

Another imaginative example of theme-based parties was the annual benefit of the Neil Bogart Memorial Fund, a music industry–based group that raises money for children's cancer, leukemia, and AIDS research. Inspired by the popular 1970s variety/talk shows, such as the ones hosted by Merv Griffin, Mike Douglas, and Dinah Shore, the creative direction for this unique event emerged with a color palette of powder blue, burnt orange, and chocolate brown and with images of rabbit-eared TVs. Merv Griffin signed on as guest host, and Ted Lange, aka Isaac of Love Boat fame, agreed to tend bar. All the necessary cultural and visual cues were in place for the perfect invitation: a die-cut TV set with its own attachable silver antenna and the instructions, "To improve your reception for this event please attach antenna." The dress code: "Pucci swirls, synthetics, bell bottoms, and dry-look hairdos."

Events related directly to an organization's mission, rather than to a specific theme, call for invitations with a strong and clear message. The Juvenile Diabetes Foundation's Los Angeles Promise Ball honored the legendary UCLA basketball coach John Wooden by focusing on Coach Wooden's philosophical "pyramid of success," not on an obvious basketball cliché. The card peeled open, layer by layer, as a series of triangles became progressively larger with each unfolding. Every panel revealed a single word that captured the organization's objective and the honoree's driving tenets: Success, Integrity, and Faith.

An even greater level of sensitivity and compassion needed to be transmitted in the work created for the National AIDS Memorial Grove. The fifteen-acre site, serenely nestled in San Francisco's Golden Gate Park, is the country's living, growing memorial dedicated to the lives touched by and lost to AIDS.

GROSGRAIN RIBBON AND HAND-DRIPPED WAX

simulated an old leather book to invite guests to the premiere of Turner Network Television's original movie *The Hunchback*.

To invite donors and friends to a twilight reception in the Memorial Grove, the invitation showed a dramatically enlarged black-and-white photograph of the Memorial Grove's centerpiece, the Circle of Friends. The flagstone area is inscribed with the names of people whose lives have been touched by the disease. A lone gladiolus, resting across someone's name, was hand-tinted in terra-cotta. Inside, nothing could have been more appropriate than the purity of Isaac Bashevis Singer's quotation: "What nature creates has eternity in it."

At times, charity and commerce unite to create events that raise money for worthy causes while also supporting business ventures. For the invitation to the unveiling of Lalique's limited-edition "Elton's Angel" (which were sold in support of the Elton John AIDS Foundation), a large amount of factual information had to be included without sacrificing the elegance of the legendary French crystal company. The result was a delicate, hand-bound paper book, edged with a spine of gold cord, containing enough pages to include the foundation's mission statement, a history of the angel, a description of the special edition, and the time, date, and location of the party.

"The pleasant place of all festivity. The revel of the earth, The masque of Italy."

Lord Byron on Venice

Ballo in Maschera
Venezia, Italia

THE ULTIMATE PARTY—
an all-expense-paid trip to a masquerade ball in Venice, Italy, required the ultimate invitations. The party began with the save-the-date card, UPPER LEFT, complete with a quote by Lord Byron and a gold-embossed question mark. The invitation, BELOW, was delivered in a sumptuous velvet-upholstered box containing a handmade imported mask and printed in Italian and English. Upon acceptance of the invitation, guests were provided with confirmation packets in velvet pouches, UPPER RIGHT, complete with travel information, accommodations, and a blank mask to decorate.

{CORPORATE EVENTS}

In an era of fierce corporate competition, many companies find that the best way to promote their image, boost morale, or cement client loyalty is through large-scale, sometimes lavish, blockbuster events. To be sure, this is not the place for unimaginative correspondence. The mark of a compelling corporate invitation is one that surprises the recipient—revealing a side of the company that is unlike the one experienced on a daily basis. This requires taking certain creative risks. The more innovative the design, the more likely it will possess "desk value"—the term I use to describe the prestige and staying power that come from an invitation prominently displayed on an executive's desk.

For a series of worldwide hundredth-anniversary celebrations that culminated with a thousand-person gala in Los Angeles, the prestigious international law firm of Gibson, Dunn & Crutcher departed from standard, black-engraved ecru cards. Instead, regal sapphire blue and pageantry red French wired ribbons bordered invitations that were penned in an elegant copperplate script and stamped with a burgundy wax seal reading "1890–1990." The double-layered ribbon also ran along the left side of the outer envelopes, a half inch from the edge, and completed the stately presentation.

Using a company's logo or official colors is important to maintain the sanctity of the established business culture, but through only slight modifications, a corporation can achieve a variety of results. For the opening of GameWorks in Las Vegas, the latest in a chain of interactive virtual-reality game arcades and restaurants, the logo was adjusted to look as if it appeared on a glimmering casino marquee. It

LALIQUE AND ELTON JOHN announced the unveiling of Elton's Angel benefiting the Elton John AIDS Foundation, ABOVE, with a beautiful book-like invitation made from heavy cotton rag stock. In celebration of the law firm Gibson, Dunn & Crutcher's hundredth anniversary, BELOW, formal invitations were sent worldwide and adorned with a double layer of French ribbon dressing the outside envelope and inside card.

COMPAQ COMPUTER'S "EVENING IN CASABLANCA"

came in the form of a leather-covered dossier with debossed designs. It was tied with a rich gold tassel and was sent in an envelope with authentic reproductions of French Moroccan stamps circa 1942.

appeared through a series of die-cut ovals that transported the viewer through the decades of Las Vegas history, from the barren desert of the 1930s, to the Nealy O'Hara showgirl glory of the 1960s, to the adult playground it has become today.

When computer giants Compaq and Microsoft cohosted a party during a trade conference in Orlando, Florida, the "Evening in Casablanca" theme overtook the Isleworth Country Club. It was a rare business affair, since no corporate logos could be found. Creating weathered, leather-covered dossiers evoked the spirit of the party in minute detail with images of a prop plane, a map indicating the route from Orlando to Casablanca, and the text, printed in sleek Art Deco–looking Parisian type, promising to

A CAMPAIGN BUTTON

added dimension on invitations for the premiere of *Kingfish,* a movie about Huey Long.

HOPE

A FILM BY GOLDIE HAWN

a special screening event

...dear things.

GOLDIE HAWN'S directorial debut, *Hope*, a TNT original movie, is the story of a young girl coming of age in the South during the racial turbulence of the early '60s. The invitation in the form of a personal diary had its own brass key, a satin moiré covering, and gold-tipped edges, and it was innocently tied with satin ribbon.

A Tribal Mask

embossed in rich metallic copper and closed with a wooden nose bone serves as the invitation, ABOVE, for BMG Entertainment's Grammy party at New York's Museum of Natural History. Dr. Seuss came alive with die-cut pop-outs of familiar characters in the invitation, BELOW, to the Hollywood premiere of *In Search of Dr. Seuss* followed by a party on the fabled "Mulberry Street" in Sony Studio's back lot.

"transport you back in time to the sands of the Sahara in far away Morocco, a land of tasty delicacies, dazzling entertainment, and Arabian surprises." An old document holder with a string-and-button closure held the dossier, while a personalized airmail label and reproductions of 1942 French Moroccan stamps decorated the exterior. The stamps, which had been laser color-copied onto label stock and die-cut with perforated edges, looked so authentic that they could have fooled the Postmaster General. To preserve the impact of the presentation, invitations were delivered via Federal Express.

Innovative materials cannot be underestimated in the way they attract attention. Few advertising and marketing tools compare to the sensory experience and "play value" that come from using a wide range of unusual tactile materials, from aluminum to zebra-patterned fake fur. Trend-setting companies will try extreme measures, from cutting-edge design to elaborate printing techniques, to achieve their marketing goals. This is especially true in the burgeoning realm of cybertechnology. To honor the world's "cyber elite"—pioneers, gurus, entrepreneurs, and moguls—*Time Digital,* Time Inc.'s magazine about everything digital, sent invitations printed on fiery orange cards with refractive vinyl that appeared three-dimensional; resistors taken directly from an electronic circuit board secured the invitations. Recipients could R.S.V.P. by telephone or via the company's Internet address—definitely the new wave in responses. In a world of voice mail, lightning-fast modems, and animated Web sites, a whole new medium is emerging to bring the art of invitations into the next millennium.

TIME DIGITAL
PRESENTS
THE CYBER ELITE

OIN TIME DIGITAL,
RLD'S MOST INFLUENTIAL
TECHNOLOGY MAGAZINE,
ING CYBERSPACE'S 50 MOST IMPORTANT
ERS, GURUS, ENTREPRENEURS, MOGUL
AND HIGH-TECH MOVERS & SHAKERS

, EDITOR,
AND TIME'S

AN ACTUAL RESISTOR,
a remnant from the dawn of the electronic age, was used to attach refractive holographic vinyl to a screaming orange and metallic silver invitation, ABOVE, for *Time Digital* magazine honoring the most influential "cyber elite." Gameworks, BELOW, a joint venture of Dreamworks SKG and Sega, combined vintage photos of the Las Vegas strip with a shimmering, glittery backdrop for their logo, to invite guests to the grand opening of their Las Vegas virtual reality, interactive eatery.

GLOSSARY
{what things mean}

blind embossing : a process that raises letters or images in paper through the use of an embossing die without the addition of ink

calligraphic hands : the various script and lettering styles that an accomplished calligrapher can produce, including distinctive informal printing, elegant, embellished italics, scripts, and historic Gothic lettering

calligraphy : the precise art of penmanship

camera-ready art : a black-and-white reproduction of an image, used for reproduction in offset lithography and various other printing processes

cast-coated : a paper finish with a very shiny, glossy, or polished reflective surface

cotton fiber : paper made from 100 percent pure cotton fiber pulp; also known as cotton rag when the pulp is created from actual cotton rags

cotton rag : (see cotton fiber)

debossing : a printing technique utilizing a die to create an indented design

deckle edge : the irregular, feathered and sometimes rough edge of handmade paper

die : an etched brass, copper, or magnesium plate that is used to create engraved, embossed, or foil-stamped images and type; the cost of dies is determined by the size and detail of the image being etched

die-cutting : the process of cutting various paper shapes, particularly for envelopes, using a steel-rule die that is similar to an old-fashioned cookie cutter

directions card : an invitation insert used strictly for difficult-to-find locations or for out-of-town guests, it can be designed in map form or printed with worded directions; the phone number of the location should always be included

embossing : a printing technique in which a sculptured brass die is used to create a design with a precise, multilayered relief surface to add dimension and texture

engraving : a printing process employed by Rembrandt and other artists for etchings, it reproduces finely detailed images from a hand-etched copper or steel die; engraved images and type are unmistakable for their slightly raised surface, which leaves a "bruise," the slight indentation on the back of the sheet of paper

engraving plate : an etched steel die that is used to create engraved type or images

escort cards : small cards, also known as table seating cards, which direct guests to their assigned tables

flourishes : the flowery and decorative calligraphic embellishments that often appear in very formal invitations or menus

foil stamping : a printing process in which metallic, pigmented, or holographic foils are imprinted on paper through the use of special printing foils and a copper or magnesium stamping die

font : (see typeface)

gatefold : a folded card that opens from the middle, rather than on one side

gifting card : an invitation insert used when a host requests a donation to a specific charity or other gift instructions; it may provide some information about the charity, such as its address and phone number

honorific : for correspondence purposes, this term refers to a person's title, including Mr., Mrs., and Dr., as well as titles for military personnel and elected officials

industrial paper :	usually made from chipboard or newsprint, it is primarily used for manufacturing or commercial purposes
initial cap :	an oversize and dramatically illuminated first letter of a word usually created by calligraphy or a decorative typeface; also know as a dropped cap
kraft paper :	industrial or recycled paper that resembles brown grocery bags
letterpress :	a printing method developed by Gutenberg in the fifteenth century where a sheet of paper is hand-fed into a letterpress machine; the lettering is formed into a metal stamping die, covered with a light layer of ink, and then pressed into paper
linen finish :	a paper finish that looks and feels like its namesake fabric
marbled paper :	a decorative paper art recognizable for distinctive overall patterns that resemble the surface of marble, traditionally used for fancy end papers or linings in hand-made books
matte :	paper with a dull, nonreflective surface or finish
mold :	a fine-screened frame used for shaping wet pulp into individual sheets of handmade paper; many paper mills still use this centuries-old process that produces papers with feathered, deckled edges and distinctive watermarks
offset lithography :	a printing process utilizing camera-ready art for quick and inexpensive copies
Pantone Matching System :	a method for specifying and insuring color consistency of thousands of ink colors and shades by a number known as a PMS color
photoengraving :	similar to engraving, photoengraving is a newer printing process that uses a die made from a chemical process of etching
point size :	the unit of measure that specifies the size of an individual letter or character; the larger the point size, the larger the letter; a one-inch letter is approximately seventy-two points
reception card :	one of many components that can be inserted into an invitation package, it tells the location and time of a reception if it takes place at a different location or time from the primary event
R.S.V.P. card :	shorthand for the French phrase "répondez s'il vous plaît," or "please reply," R.S.V.P. cards are sent along with invitations for a response by mail
save-the-date card :	a simple postcard or a shorthand version of an invitation mailed long in advance of an event that notifies guests to hold a particular date for an event and usually includes the words "Details to follow"; such notices are helpful when the host has not yet firmed up all the details or is beginning the planning at a very late date
stock :	a term that refers to the paper component of a project
thermography :	a printing process using a combination of heat and thermography powders that gives images a raised surface similar to that made from engraving but without the bruise and fine detail; it is also known as thermo engraving
typeface :	the general term that refers to the style of a letter or numeral; the characteristics of type styles are serif, sans serif, script, block, italic, or bold (with the advent of desktop publishing the term *typeface* is used interchangeably with *font*)
typesetting :	the process of setting typefaces by computer or machine; letters individually cast in metal and hand-set by a typographer for a printing press are no longer used; today, most typesetting is computer generated with thousands of fonts available
vellum :	paper that is frosted and translucent; in medieval times, vellum was made from the treated skins of calves or lambs and was similar to parchment
virgin paper :	paper that is made from pure, unused pulp and does not contain recycled fiber content
watermark :	the signature or emblem embedded into paper that is visible when the paper is held up to the light

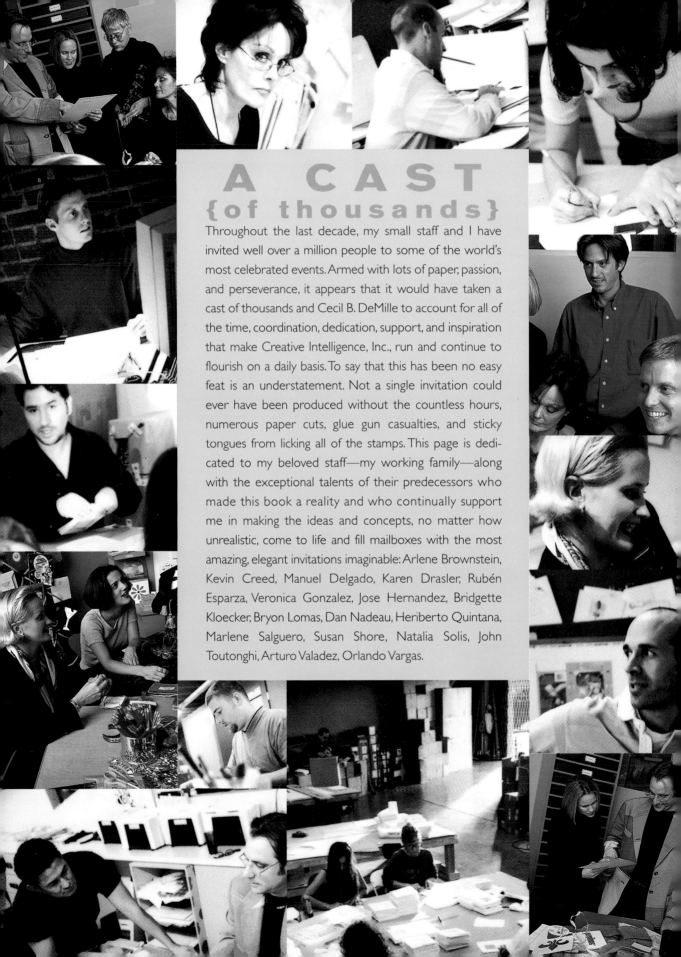

A CAST
{of thousands}

Throughout the last decade, my small staff and I have invited well over a million people to some of the world's most celebrated events. Armed with lots of paper, passion, and perseverance, it appears that it would have taken a cast of thousands and Cecil B. DeMille to account for all of the time, coordination, dedication, support, and inspiration that make Creative Intelligence, Inc., run and continue to flourish on a daily basis. To say that this has been no easy feat is an understatement. Not a single invitation could ever have been produced without the countless hours, numerous paper cuts, glue gun casualties, and sticky tongues from licking all of the stamps. This page is dedicated to my beloved staff—my working family—along with the exceptional talents of their predecessors who made this book a reality and who continually support me in making the ideas and concepts, no matter how unrealistic, come to life and fill mailboxes with the most amazing, elegant invitations imaginable: Arlene Brownstein, Kevin Creed, Manuel Delgado, Karen Drasler, Rubén Esparza, Veronica Gonzalez, Jose Hernandez, Bridgette Kloecker, Bryon Lomas, Dan Nadeau, Heriberto Quintana, Marlene Salguero, Susan Shore, Natalia Solis, John Toutonghi, Arturo Valadez, Orlando Vargas.

ACKNOWLEDGMENTS
{with a million thanks}

The creation of this book has been an extraordinary experience. It has been a living workshop complete with great lessons in patience, perseverance, and trust in the simple, overwhelming, richly emotional, amazing process called creativity. This book has had a life of its own from the very beginning, starting with my agent, **Al Lowman**, who followed his instinct to seek me out and make this book a reality, and culminating with **Lauren Shakely**, at Clarkson N. Potter, who was unwavering in her support and belief in my talent. The unbelievable team at Clarkson N. Potter was awesome, making my first publishing experience a complete joy, including art director **Marysarah Quinn**, with gentle but firm insistence that I follow my gut with matters of style and form; **Kathryn Crosby**, always conscientious and editorially savvy; and **Wendy Schuman**, marketing and public relations whiz, whose excitement and passion for this project were made clear before this book was even published. And a special thanks to the marketing and sales staff at Clarkson Potter. **B.G. Dilworth** and **Charlotte Patton** of Authors and Artists Group were absolute gems every step along the way.

I feel blessed to have had the finest creative team possible: **Susan Salinger**, who shot all of the remarkably stunning, captivating photographs, and **Valorie Hart**, angel, creative midwife, resident mom, director of photography, and all-around style meister, who pulled the project together in every which way possible. And then there is **Betty Goodwin**, who not only organized and cowrote the text, but captured my voice through each and every carefully chosen word. **Bridgette Kloecker** and **Bryon Lomas**, the shining stars of my art department, after a full day of demanding work, found enough energy to continue working throughout the wee hours to design, revise, design, and revise in accordance with my ever-changing ideas and inspirations. I am so proud of them. And an extra special thank-you to **Sherry Schlossberg**, who is constantly reinventing what's possible with a calligrapher's pen and ink. My very dear friend **Andrea King** provided her home filled with almost every conceivable element required to prop the photography. **Randy Franks**, specializing in matters of style, provided the additional objets d'art that only he could conjure up.

Susan Shore, Arlene Brownstein, John Toutonghi, Kevin Creed, Arturo Valadez, and **Dan Nadeau**, the talented and inexhaustible crew at Creative Intelligence, handled all of the administrative coordination, from clearances to pulling and organizing archives. **Dina Chernick, Shari Creed, Richard Brickman, Ted Kruckel, Judy Schonfeld**, and **Lori Posner**, the extended support team at CI, provided their respective counsel on almost every matter from style to public relations and the legalities of it all. Before this book became a reality, there were several individuals whose work helped make the project come to life—**Denise Abbott**, for her wonderfully penned piece in <u>InStyle Magazine,</u> **Martha Nelson**, editor-in-chief of <u>InStyle</u>, for her constant and unending support. **JoAnne Jaffe, Jeannine Stein, Pelig Top, Emily Gwathmey**, and **Jean Penn** all gave their help in the very beginning. Providing comfort along the way was **Keith Klevan** and son **Aaron** who allowed Mom to work weekends; **Alberto Paz**, **Larry Sexton**, and **Timothy Pope**, who led me to Valorie. **Sylvia Litter**, **Michael LaRiche**, **Monica Morant**, and **Welch Golightly** were a huge help with photography assistance and copy art. I also want to acknowledge the overwhelming kindness, guidance, and professional support of **Sarah Shirley**, **Carol Celluci**, and **Deborah Kelman**. I am fortunate to have had the opportunity to work with some of the nation's most talented party mavens, caterers, and florists who conceive, coordinate, produce, and cater the most magnificent events: **Colin Cowie** and **Stuart Brownstein**, **Mary Micucci** and her staff at Along Came Mary, **Terri DePaolo**, **Carl Bendix**, **David Corwin**, **Ina Poncher**, **Kimm Birkicht** of the Velvet Garden, **Sharon Sacks**, Susan Holland, **Walter Hubert**, **Stanlee Gatti**, **Paula Le Duc**, **Suzanne Lemay**, **Carlotta Florio**, **Paul Cunliffe** and Merv Griffin Productions, **Wendy Creed**, **Toby Cox**, **Mark Yumkas**, **Tom Byrne**, and **Jeanne Berry**.

Perhaps my most heartfelt thanks goes to my clients, the most creatively inspired people on the planet, who have made my work possible: Oprah Winfrey, Lyndie and Kenny G, Kate and Steven Spielberg, Elizabeth Nye, Rita and Tom Hanks, Molly Avery, Quincy Jones, Debborah Foreman, Jolie Jones, Lisa, Dustin, and Becky Hoffman, Carrie Fisher, Kathleen Kennedy and Frank Marshall, Mary Radford, Ruth and Elliot Handler, Betty and Fred Hayman, Inez Walters, Sharon Summerall and Don Henley, Gina Cefalu, Anne and Nicholas Holt, Joley Fisher, Michele and Michael Bernstein, Cindy Costner, Anita Phillips, Compaq Computer, John Shea, Gameworks, Alschuler Grossman & Pines, Margaret, Howard, and Armen Weitzman, Jane Bay, Lauren and Arthur Levine, Stacey and Henry Winkler, Craig Donahue, Patti Maloney, Rikki and Fred Rosen, Marilyn and Jeffrey Katzenberg, Ben Donnenberg, John Giurini, Karen and Stan Winston, Kerry Enright, Maria and Kenneth Cole, Bernadette and Ray Leonard, Alice Russell Shapiro, Margaret and Willard Carr, Edd Stepp, Gibson, Dunn, & Crutcher, Jeff and Margo Baker Barbakow, Barbara Lutton, Deborah Le Vine, Scot Safon, Laura Dames, Kim Kleinman, Da Vida Rice, Deloris Horn, Priscilla Valldejuli, Kim Freedman, Susie Field, Bonnie Kyle, Audrey Pass, Herman Leonard, Irma Bueno, Merrill Morrison, Phyllis Hennigan, Chris Kitrinos, Susan Pierson, P.G.A., Dan Osheyack, Keisha and Forest Whitaker, Barbara Lazaroff, Francis Kidd, Jill and Brad Grey.

Extra special thanks to Karen Carbone, Susie Zegan, Pediatric AIDS Foundation, Susan Lietz, Joyce Bogart and the Neil Bogart Memorial Fund, Sandy Pressman, Bill Melamed, Joan Borinstein, Scott Sanders, and the Museum of Contemporary Art, who have been with me since the beginning. And, of course, standing by my side at all times are my friends Judy Sitzer, Dora Graye, Bruce Roberts, Allison Robbins and Jim Jennewein, Merle Ellias, Nancy Schiff, Dennis Erdman, Paul Burditch, Bari Mattes and Michael O'Brien, Liz Heller, Mindi Horwitch, Barbara Gortikov, and Harvey Siegel. The Friedland clan—**Jean**; **Jay**, **Cyndy**, and **Justin**; **Adrienne**, **Seth**, **Evan**, and **Jordan**—provided unconditional support, and **Luvee** too, even though she's "just a dog." And to my very best friend, **Darren Star**,—who has been by my side from the very beginning—words could never fully express my gratitude for the greatest gift of all—your friendship, clarity, and love.

I sincerely thank you all so very much for your patronage and support —Marc

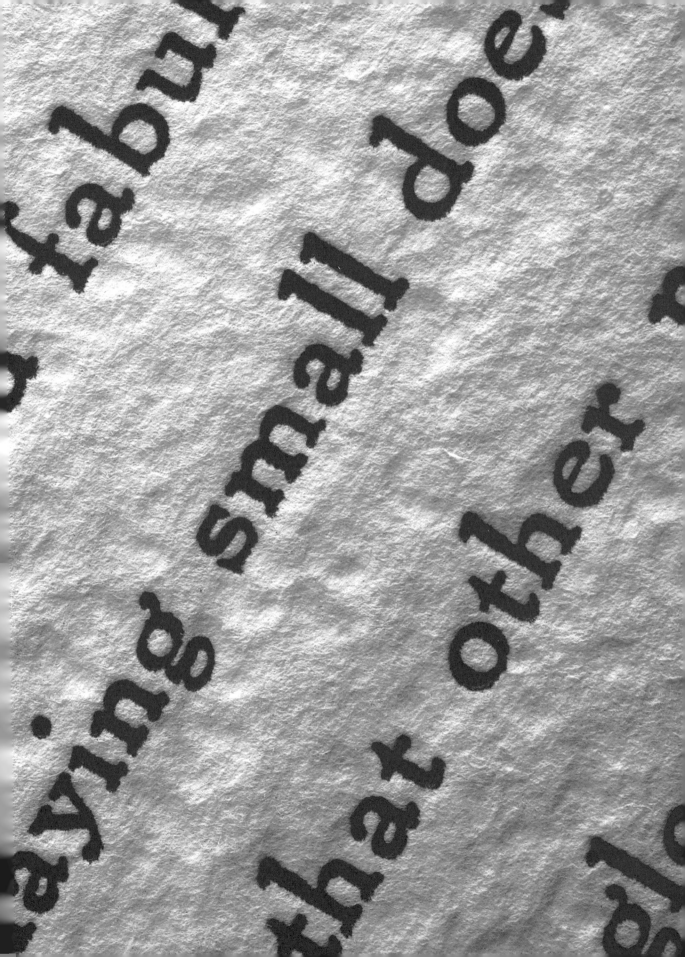